G000297470

Landscapes of
CYPRUS

a countryside guide
Seventh edition

Geoff Daniel
revised and updated by
Mark George and Jane Mead

SUNFLOWER BOOKS

Seventh edition
Copyright © 2016
Sunflower Books™
P O Box 36160
London SW7 3WS, UK

ISBN 978-1-85691-482-6

In the Troodos Mountains

Important note to the reader

We have tried to ensure that the descriptions and maps in this book are error-free at press date. Travellers to Cyprus will be aware of changes to the names of major towns and cities — Lefkosia for Nicosia, Lemesos for Limassol. This is part of official moves to create a stronger national identity in the Greek part of the island. We have incorporated the major changes, but you will no doubt encounter others. This book will be updated, where necessary, whenever future printings permit. Sunflower will be happy to receive your comments for updating, preferably sent by e-mail to www.sunflowerbooks.co.uk.

   We also rely on those who use this book — especially walkers — to take along a good supply of common sense when they explore. Conditions change fairly rapidly on Cyprus, and *storm damage or bulldozing may make a route unsafe at any time*. If the route is not as we outline it here, and your way ahead is not secure, return to the point of departure. *Never attempt to complete a tour or walk under hazardous conditions!* Please read carefully the notes on pages 19 and 41 to 48, as well as the introductory comments at the beginning of each tour and walk (regarding road conditions, equipment, grade, distances and time, etc). Explore *safely*, while at the same time respecting the beauty of the countryside.

Cover photograph: Akamas Peninsula
Title page: In the Troodos Mountains

Photographs: 25 (top), 29 (bottom right), 30, 85 (top), 95 (bottom),
   106-107, 113: John and Christine Oldfield; 32, 36, 40, 61 (top):
   istock photo; 72 (top), 95 (top), 97 (bottom): Pat Underwood; 52,
   57, 64 (middle): Mark George; cover: Shutterstock; all other photo-
   graphs: the author
Maps and plans: Sunflower Books
Drawings: Katharina Kelly
A CIP catalogue record for this book is available from the British
   Library.
Printed and bound in England: Short Run Press, Exeter

Contents

3

4 Landscapes of Cyprus

Lakki harbour

Preface _____

Cyprus, birthplace of the mythical love goddess Aphrodite, yields its greatest pleasures to the visitor who makes an effort towards closer acquaintance.

If you are content with sun, sand, surf and soured brandy, then you won't be disappointed. But deeper exploration of this special island, on foot or on wheels, coupled with a healthy curiosity about its people and its traditions, will reward you with experiences to treasure for a lifetime. Should your first visit to Cyprus be the start of an incurable love affair, do not be at all surprised!

This Sixth edition of *Landscapes of Cyprus* is divided into three main sections, each with its own introduction.

For **motorists**, there are car tours taking in lively resorts, picturesque villages, mountain spectacle, fast new roads and very slow old ones. There are suggestions for 4WD enthusiasts, too.

Picnickers can take their choice of authorised sites with benches and barbecue facilities, or out-of-the-way locations along the route of a walk.

Walkers have a comprehensive guide to Cyprus on foot, totally revised and updated. The walks cover most areas of the island, most are within the stride of anyone sound in wind and limb, and most are easily accessible.

Cyprus — past

The turbulent history of Cyprus dates back to the Stone Age, and the island has undergone numerous changes of 'ownership' over the centuries. Turks, Romans, Greeks, Venetians, and the British have all played a part in the island's destiny. In Lefkosia the Cyprus Museum and the Museum of National Struggle are well worth visiting to gain an appreciation of the past.

Throughout the island, richly historic sites beckon the curious traveller, not least the imposing 13th-century castle at Kolossi, Lefkosia's Venetian walls, the ancient Tombs of the Kings at Pafos, and the Neolithic settlement at Khirokitia.

In the mountainous Troodos region, nine churches on UNESCO's World Heritage list are rightly famous for beautiful frescoes painted between the 11th and 15th centuries.

Cyprus — present

Cyprus has been an independent republic within the British Commonwealth since 1960, joining the EU in 2004. In 1974 Turkey occupied the northern and north-eastern regions (some 36% of the island; see the fold-out map), establishing a state which remains unrecognised in the international community. For the past decade, however, it has been possible to travel freely between the two sectors: see pages 20-21. While *Landscapes of Cyprus* regrettably confines its coverage to the south of the still-divided island, those wishing to enjoy the best walks in the north can do so with Sunflower's guide *Walk & Eat North Cyprus* — while sampling delicious food along the way.

Cyprus — people

For all their upheavals, Greek Cypriots remain among the most cheerful, gregarious and hospitable folk you could ever meet. English is widely understood, but even a stumbling attempt at a few words of Greek (see page 47) on the part of the visitor is warmly appreciated. Cypriot hospitality is legendary — *kopiaste!* (come in and join us!) — and should always be accepted, even if sparingly.

Cyprus — environment

Walking, and other leisure activities which respect the island's somewhat fragile environment, will become increasingly important as conventional coast-based tourism heads towards saturation point. The creation of a national park in the beautiful Akamas region in the west was a positive move to ensure protection of sensitive areas such as the green turtle nesting grounds at Lara Beach.

Acknowledgements

My thanks to John and Christine Oldfield, authors of Sunflower guides to the Costa Blanca and Andalucia, for fieldwork on the Fourth edition, to the Sunflower team for revising the Fifth and Sixth editions, but particularly to Mark George and Jane Mead who rewalked most of the routes for this Seventh edition and contributed two new walks. *Do* visit their website for even more island walks: www.cypruswalks.net.

Books

Landscapes of Cyprus is a guide to countryside exploration, intended to be used in addition to a general guide. Christos Georgiades' *Nature of Cyprus — environment, flora and fauna*, available on the island, is a valuable pictorial reference; Colin Thubron's *Journey into Cyprus*, an account of a pre-1974 walk round the island, is a scholarly but absorbing read; and Lawrence Durrell's classic, *Bitter Lemons*, is an amusing and poignant portrait of a Cyprus long gone. To discover the best walks and tours in northern Cyprus, see Sunflower's *Walk & Eat North Cyprus.*

Getting about

A **hired car** is undoubtedly the most practical way of exploring Cyprus. Numerous companies offer a wide range of vehicles, from runabouts to prestige models. Small 4WD soft-tops are very popular, and their modest extra cost is worth considering if you plan trips into the mountains or remote regions — such is the rough condition of many minor road surfaces. I have included some 4WD route suggestions in this book.

Coach tours operate from the main tourist centres, and offer a painless introduction to road conditions and a comfortable view of island scenery.

Intercity buses are an inexpensive way of moving from one place to another, perhaps for tackling a walk out of a different centre from your hotel base.

Taxis operate in profusion in the towns, more sparsely in villages, and all are identified by a prefix 'T' to the registration number. Rates are fixed by the authorities, and urban taxis are obliged to operate a meter on all journeys. Fares are not high, but on longer journeys it is wise to agree a price in advance. In town you will likely ride in a new Mercedes, but in a village it will probably be something older and more interesting!

Service taxis are a useful way of getting from town to town if you're not in a hurry. They ply between major centres approximately every half-hour and will pick you up at your hotel and take you anywhere central at your destination, picking up and dropping off other passengers en route. They are useful on walks which end on a service taxi route: just ask a bar or café owner to request a taxi stop on its next run. Rates are very cheap for the service offered. You will share your trip with other passengers (possibly in a minibus), but this is the only inconvenience.

Local buses are usually not very helpful for the walker; essentially they bring village folk to town in early morning and take them home later in the day.

Service taxi and bus timetables are given on pages 121-133, but *do collect an up-to-date timetable* from the nearest tourist office as soon as you arrive on Cyprus or, better still, log on to www.cyprusbybus.com before you go, where you can seach all local and intercity bus routes, bus stops and timetables by area, with interactive maps.

8   Landscapes of Cyprus

LEFKOSIA
(Nicosia)

1   Tourist Information
2   Post Office
3   Municipal Library
4   Town Hall
5   Municipal Museum (of History)
6   Museum of the National Struggle
7   St John's Cathedral
8   Archbishop's Palace and Makarios Cultural Centre
9   Municipal Cultural Centre
10 Police Station
11 Cyprus Archaeological Museum
12 Telephones
13 Municipal Theatre
14 House of Representatives
15 Hospital
16 British High Commission
17 Cyprus Airways
18 US Embassy
19 Presidential Palace
20 Liberty Monument
21 Bayraktar Mosque
22 Museum of Contemporary Art
23 Omeriye Mosque
24 Trypiotis Church
25 Chrysaliniotissa Church/ Chrysaliniotissa Crafts Centre
26 Faneromeni Church
27 Ledra Palace
🚖 Travel & Express (Cyprus Interurban Taxi Co —Service Taxis)
🚌 Bus 'Station' (Solomos Square)
▬   Crossing Points for North Cyprus

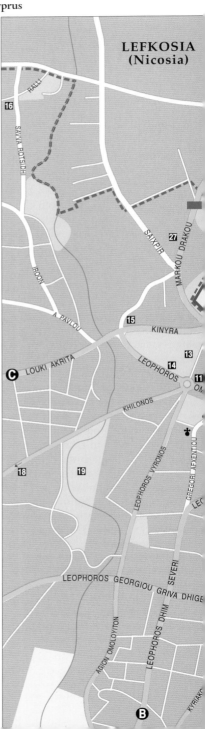

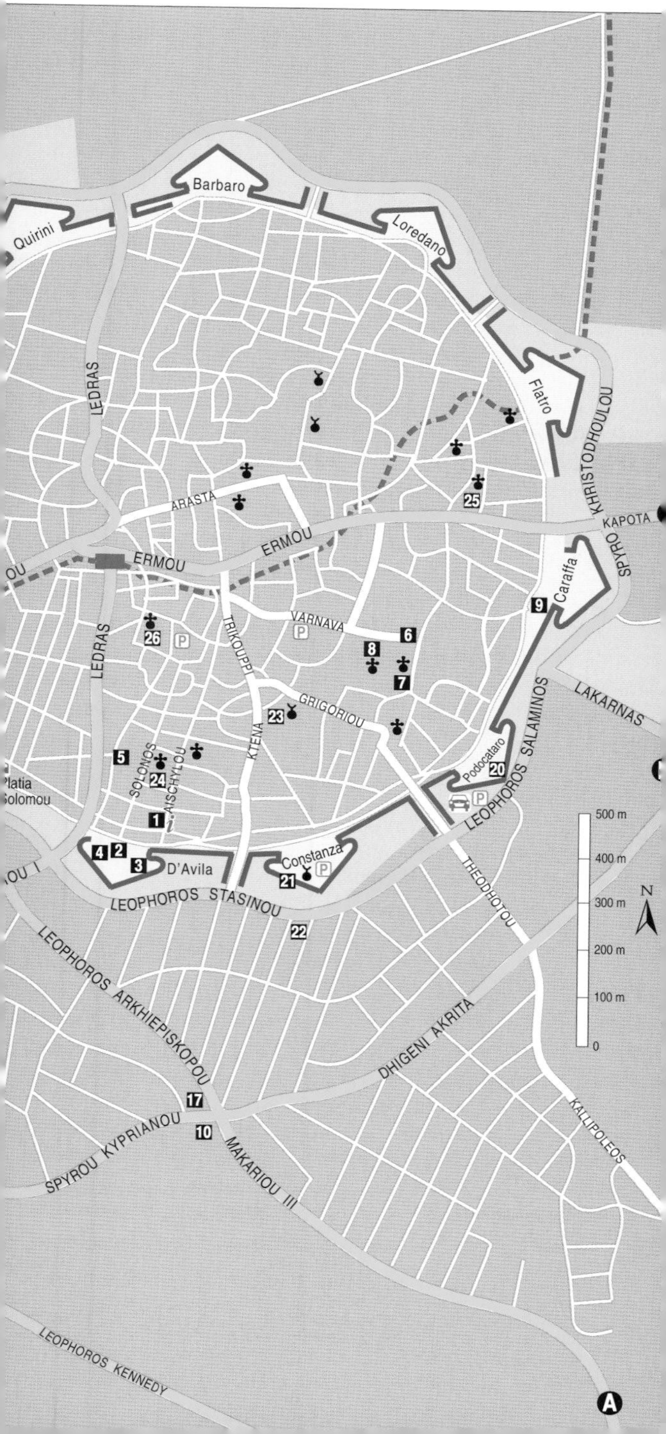

Quirini

Barbaro

Loredano

Filatro

LEDRAS

ARASTA

ERMOU

ERMOU

KHRISTODHOULOU

SPYRO KAPOTA

25

Carafia

26

9

LEDRAS

TRIKOUPI

VARNAVA

6

8

7

GRIGORIOU

23

LAKARNAS

LEOPHOROS SALAMINOS

5

SOLONOS

24

LYSCHYLOU

KTENA

Platia Solomou

1

Podocataro

20

4 2

3

D'Avila

Constanza

21

THEODHOTOU

OU I

LEOPHOROS STASINOU

22

500 m

400 m

LEOPHOROS ARKHIEPISKOPOU

DHIGENI AKRITA

300 m

200 m

100 m

N

0

SPYROU KYPRIANOU

17

10

MAKARIOU III

KALLIPOLEOS

SPYROU KYPRIANOU

LEOPHOROS KENNEDY

A

PAFOS (Paphos)

9   Telephones
10 Bishop's Palace
11 Byzantine Museum
12 Ethnographical Museum
13 Post Office
14 Agia Solomoni Catacomb
15 Ruined Theatre
16 Odeon and Agora
17 Aquarium
18 Frankish Baths
19 Dionysos Houses (Mosaics)

20 Byzantine Fortress
21 St Paul's Pillar
22 Early Basilica (Ruins)
23 Customs House
24 Pafos Castle
25 Medieval Fort (Ruin)

PAFOS (Paphos)

1   Tourist Information
2   Cyprus Airways
3   Market
4   Police Station
5   Stadium
6   Library
7   Markedeio Theatre
8   Town Hall

🚌 Travel & Express (Cyprus Interurban Taxi Co — Service Taxis)
🚌1 Karavella Bus Station
🚌2 Kato Pafos Bus 'Station'

LARNAKA (Larnaca)

1   Tourist Information
2   Post Office
3   Municipal Cultural Centre
4   Police Station
5   Pierides Museum (Archaeology)
6   Archaeological Museum
7   Acropolis of Kition
8   Tennis Courts
9   Phoenician Temple
10 Mycenean Walls
11 Kimon Statue
12 Hospital
13 Customs Office
14 Municipal Teatre
15 Natural History Museum
16 Municipal Library
17 Telephones
18 Stadium
19 Cyprus Airways
20 Cultural/Sports Centre
21 Medieval Fort (Museum)
22 Agia Phaneromeni
23 Agios Lazarus
24 Market
🚌 Travel & Express (Cyprus Interurban Taxi Co — Service Taxis)
🚌1 Bus 'Station' (Phinikoudes)
🚌2 Osea buses

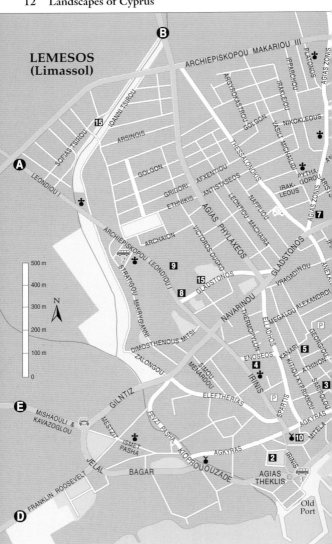

LEMESOS (Limassol)

1 Tourist Information
2 Castle and Museum
3 Town Hall
4 Bishop's Seat and Church
5 Market
6 Telephones
7 Municipal Theatre
8 Police Headquarters
9 Hospital
10 Great Mosque (Kebir)
11 Cathedral
12 Library and Cultural Centre
13 Open-AirTheatre and Zoo
14 Archaeological Museum
15 Post Offices
16 Cyprus Airways
17 Art Museums
🚍 Travel & Express (Cyprus Interurban Taxi Co — Service Taxis)
🚌1 Intercity Buses
🚌2 EMEL Central Station
🚌3 to EMEL Lambrou Porfir Station (650m/yds)

AGIA NAPA

1 Tourist Information
2 Post Office
3 Open-Air Theatre/Town
4 Agia Napa Monastery
5 Police Station
6 Municipal (Sea) Museum
🚌1 Intercity Bus Stop
🚌2 Osea Bus Stop

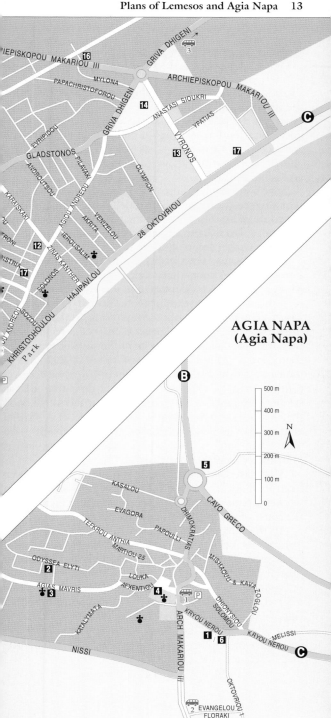

ARHIEPISKOPOU MAKARIOU III

16

MYLONA

PAPACHRISTOFOROU

GRIVA DHIGENI

3

GRIVA DHIGENI

ARCHIEPISKOPOU MAKARIOU III

C

14

ANASTASI SIOUKRI

VYRONOS

YPATIAS

EVRIPIDOU

13

17

GLADSTONOS

PILAVAKI

OLYMPION

ANDROUTSOU

AGIOU ANDREOU

AKRITA

VENIZELOU

28 OKTOVRIOU

KARAISKAKI

IEROUSALIM

TRON

12

ZINAS KANTHER

PISTRIA

17

SOLONOS

HAJIPAVLOU

ANDREOU

SOZOU

KHRISTODHOULOU

P a r k

P

**AGIA NAPA
(Agia Napa)**

B

500 m

400 m

300 m

200 m

N

100 m

0

5

KASALOU

CAVO GRECO

EVAGORA

DHIMOKRATIAS

PAPOULLI

TEFKROU ANTHIA

MARTIOU 25

MISHAOULI & KAVA ZOGLOU

ODYSSEA ELYTI

2

LOUKA

AFXENTIOU

4

DHIONYSIOU SOLOMOU

AGIAS MAVRIS

3

1

P

KATALYMATA

ARCH MAKARIOU III

KRYOU NEROU

1 **6**

KRYOU NEROU MELISSI

NISSI

C

OKTOVRIOU

2 EVANGELOU
FLORAKI

Picnicking

Picnicking is great fun on Cyprus, not least for Cypriots themselves, who will happily tuck into an outdoor feast, especially at weekends or on festival days. This enthusiasm does not extend to walking for pleasure, however, so you are most likely to come across groups of local families enjoying an outing at an official site which is easily accessible by car.

Such a site might suit your requirements — or you may prefer to seek out somewhere much more secluded along the route of a walk. Much of the island is open countryside, but it is a matter of common sense and courtesy not to picnic within any obvious fencing or boundary.

Official sites: The Cyprus Tourism Organisation and Forestry Department have established about 30 sites. Many of them are concentrated in the Troodos mountain region, but there are excellent sites dotted all around the island. The best sites offer car parking, toilet facilities, drinking water, tables and benches, barbecue facilities and play areas for children. At some of the smaller sites in less visited areas, facilities might be minimal. Official sites are indicated in the car touring notes and on the fold-out touring map by the symbol (⋔). Remember that in winter and early spring many will be inaccessible, since they lie along rough mountain roads. A leaflet describing all these sites and a few official camp sites (the only places where camping is allowed) is available from tourist information centres on the island.

Alternative suggestions: If you prefer a picnic 'away from it all', or if you find official sites crowded (likely at weekends and in high summer), you could picnic along the route of one of the walks in this book.

All the information you need to get to one of these 'private' picnics is given on the following pages, *where picnic numbers correspond to walk numbers*, so that you can quickly find the general location by looking at the pull-out touring map (on which the area of each walk is shown in green within a white circle). I include transport details (🚌: how to get there by bus; 🚗: where to park if you come by car or taxi), how long a walk you'll have *each way*, and views or setting. Beside the picnic title you'll find a map reference: the exact location of the picnic spot is

14

shown on this *walking* map by the symbol **P**. Finally, to help you choose the right setting, many of the picnic spots are illustrated.

Please remember that these 'alternative' picnic places are generally off the beaten track: you will need to wear sensible shoes and almost certainly a sunhat (the symbol ⊃ at the right of a picnic title indicates a *picnic place in full sun*).

If travelling to your picnic by service taxi or bus, please be sure to collect an up-to-date transport timetable with operators' telephone numbers from a tourist information office or download one in advance of your visit.

If travelling to your picnic by hired car, watch out for animals and children on country roads and drive especially carefully through narrow village streets. Do park well off the road — without damaging plants — and *never* block a road or track.

All picnickers should read the country code on page 19 and go quietly in the countryside.

1 MOUNT OLYMPUS (map pages 54-55, Troodos photographs on pages 1, 51 and 56)

by car: 45min on foot   by bus: 45min on foot

🚗: park as for Walk 1 on page 49.

🚌: to/from Troodos; recheck times, and make sure there is a suitable return!

From Troodos, follow Walk 1 along the Atalante trail for the first 3km, to an open area where there are numerous picnicking possibilities in pleasant surroundings and with extensive views. On the Artemis trail (the Alternative walk) there are also plenty of benches with stunning views where picnics can be enjoyed.

2 MAKRYA KONTARKA (map pages 54-55, photograph page 56)

by car: 15-50min on foot   by bus: 15-50min on foot

🚗 and 🚌: as Picnic 1 above

From Troodos, take the Persephone nature trail from the southern end of the main street as described in Walk 2 for 15 minutes, to the group of benches among tall pines shown on page 56. This is a cool spot, but a picnic at the end of the trail (Makrya Kontarka; 50min), with magnificent views, is highly recommended, although there is little shade.

3 CALEDONIAN FALLS (map pages 54-55, photograph page 53)

by car: 5-45min on foot   by bus: about 1h10 on foot

🚗: park near the signposted Caledonian Falls nature trail, by the side of a rough road that leads from a point slightly west of Psilon Dhendron (see map for car symbol). From here it's a five minute walk to the falls. Or park at the trout farm and follow the trail up to the falls, or find a suitable place to sit beside the Kryos River within a shorter distance.

🚌: to/from Platres and walk uphill to Psilon Dhendron to begin

shady trees, pleasant ferns; very crowded in season and at weekends!

4 MESAPOTAMOS/ALMYROLIVADO/KAMBOS TOU LIVADIOU (map pages 54-55)

by car: up to 10min on foot   *by bus: not practical*
🚌: park at Mesapotamos Monastery or one of the sites on the B9 east of Troodos (Car tour 5). Mesapotamos is no longer on the Walk 4 route because the path to it has disappeared, but it *is* worth a visit.
These are wooded, shady settings. There are organised sites, but 'unofficial settings nearby — lovely places to stroll.

5 ABOVE PSILON DHENDRON (map pages 54-55)

by car or taxi: 6min on foot   *by bus: 30min on foot*
🚌 to Psilon Dhendron or 🚐 to Platres (see Picnic 3) and walk uphill to Psilon Dhendron
Follow Walk 5 for 6min, to a bench set on a rise to your right. Lovely views down to Platres and the trout farm and up to the mountains; ample shade.

7 MADHARI RIDGE (map pages 62-63, photograph page 64)

by car: 15-40min on foot   *by bus: not practical*
🚌: park near the start of the nature trail described in Walk 7.
From the nature trail information board, climb to the bench at the 15min-point for a short walk offering superb views over Kyperounda village; or follow Walk 7 for about 40 minutes, to the clearing with views over the Mesaoria Plain and towards Mount Adelphi.

8 PERA PEDI (map page 65)

by car: just 1min on foot   *by bus: not practical*
🚌: park in Pera Pedi
Follow Walk 8 to the Kryos River; a lovely peaceful area has been created, with benches, plenty of shade and the sound of running water.

10 MOUNT TRIPYLOS (map page 69, nearby photograph page 70)

by car: 40min on foot   *by bus: not accessible*
🚌: park at the Dhodheka Anemi junction (the 55km-point in Car tour 3, page 28), or park at Cedar Valley.
See Walk 10, page 69: it's 2.5km to the top of Mount Tripylos from Dhodheka Anemi, 2km from the picnic area at Cedar Valley. The ascent is the same from both (about 250m/820ft). There's a fire-watch station at the peak, and a small picnic area in a lovely setting.

12 KATHIKAS SPRING (map page 73, photograph page 25)

by car: 20min on foot   *by bus: not practical*
🚌: park at Kathikas (the 27km-point in Car tour 1).
Follow Walk 12 to the 20min-point. This is a tranquil setting with a shady bench and a spring (operate the pump by a handle on the right).

13 MAVROKOLYMBOS DAM (map and nearby photograph page 75)

by car: up to 15min on foot   *by bus: not practical*
🚌: park near the dam, on the Akoursos road (signposted off the main Pafos–Coral Bay road).
You'll find ample quiet spots on the banks of this irrigation reservoir.

14 LARA BEACH (map pages 79-78, photograph opposite) ○

by car or boat: up to 10min on foot   *by bus: not accessible*
🚌: park at Lara Beach or take a 🚤 from Pafos (see Walk 14, page 76)
A quiet undeveloped beach with a single, seasonal restaurant

Lara Beach (Picnic 14)

18a ALEKHTORA VALLEY VIEWS (map page 88) ○

by car: no walking or up to 45min on foot   *by bus:* not practical

🚗: park well off the road near the 'Alekhtora' sign and fruit packing factory at the start of Walk 18 (page 86) — or park further up the track. *Follow Walk 18 to the 45min-point (some picnickers drive most of the way). Go up on to the antenna platform and walk 50m past the antenna. Choose a spot on the right — on the grass or the rocks — overlooking the valley. No shade.*

18b KHAPOTAMI GORGE OVERLOOK (map page 88) ○

by car: up to 1h08min on foot   *by bus:* not practical

🚗: park as for Picnic 18a above.
Follow Walk 18 to the 1h08min-point, at the edge of the rocky terracing. As long as you don't mind dodging the goat droppings, this is a spectacular site. No shade.

20 'APHRODONIS' TRAIL (map on reverse of touring map, photograph page 92)

by car, or by bus and taxi: up to 1h10min on foot

🚗: park near the restaurant at the Baths of Aphrodite.
🚌 from Pafos to Polis; then bus or taxi to the Baths
There are numerous lovely spots on the first, shared part of the two trails; the benches at trail point 11 (35min) are ideal, as is the shady hollow by Pyrgos tis Rigaenas (1h10min).

21 SMIGIES (map on reverse of touring map)

by car: no walking, or up to about 2h on foot   *by bus:* not practical

🚗: park at the picnic site; the rough road is motorable in a standard car in dry weather. Or park in Neo Chorio and walk (50min each way).
A well-sited picnic area, with water, tables and benches; several short walk opportunities in the immediate vicinity (see page 94 and map).

22 DROUSSEIA (map page 96) ○

by car: 20min on foot   *by bus:* not practical

🚗: park behind the hotel in Drousseia (see *Alternative* walk, page 96)
Follow Alternative walk 22 to the 25min-point. A narrow path leads to the giant rocks. There is little shade, but fantastic views across to the Troodos, Mount Olympus, Polis Bay and the north coast.

23 MILIOU (map page 99) ○

by car: 25min uphill on foot   *by bus: not practical*
🚗: park as for Walk 23 (page 98)
*Follow the Short walk to the junction at the 25min-point. Sit on rocks near
the track junction, with panoramic views. No shade.*

25a FISHERMAN'S TRAIL (map and photograph pages 104-107)

by car: 2-10min on foot   *by bus: not practical*
🚗: park at the signposted nature trail (see Short walk, page 103)
*Picnic spots abound on this nature trail — at the water's edge (limited shade)
or at the hilltop shelter (shade, benches, fine views)*

25b A VIEW FOR THE GODS (map pages 104-105, photograph pages 106-107)

by car: 1h04min uphill on foot   *by bus: not accessible*
🚗: park as for Alternative walk 1 on page 103
*Follow Walk 25 from the 31min-point to the 4-way junction at the 1h18min-
point. Take the track straight ahead, up to a hexagonal shelter. Views in all
directions give you a matchless panorama — from Mount Olympus in the
north to the Germasogia Dam in the south, Kouklia in the west and the
mountains above Larnaka in the east. Benches to sit on, shade.*

27 STAVROVOUNI (map page 110, photos pages 37 and 111) ○

by car: 5min on foot   *by bus: not practical*
🚗: park just below the monastery.
*From the top of this striking pedestal you have a panoramic view of Cyprus.
Women are not allowed in the monastery, but views from the car park are
equally impressive. Toilets; sometimes a fruit stall.*

28 NEAR KITI TOWER (map page 112, nearby photo page 113) ○

by car: 56min on foot (or 8min if you drive as far as the watchtower)
by bus: 56min on foot
🚗 or 🚌 to Kiti
*Follow Walk 28 to the 56min-point and pick your spot on this quiet, pebbly
beach. Limited shade, lots of salty water!*

29 EAST OF AGIA NAPA (map pages 116-117, photographs pages 117 and 118) ○

by car: 5-40min on foot   *by bus: 15-40min on foot*
🚗: park at Agia Napa near the start of Walk 29 (see page 115).
🚌: check Agia Napa region times and routes at a tourist office.
*The early stages of Walk 29 offer numerous picnic opportunities, the best sand
being at Kermia Beach (no shade). Head straight there by car if you do not
wish to walk.*

30 AGII SARANTA (map map pages 116-117, photograph page 120)

by car: 20min on foot   *by bus: not practical*
🚗: park short of the transmitter tower, then walk round to Agii Saranta
as described in Short walk 30 on page 119.
*A pleasant location in the shadow of the unusual little church shown on page
120, set on a hill in the quiet agricultural area inland from the lively resort
of Agia Napa.*

A country code for walkers and motorists

The experienced rambler is used to following a 'country code' on his walks, but the tourist out for a lark can unwittingly cause damage, harm animals and even endanger his own life. Please heed the hints below.

- **Do not light fires**, except in the areas provided at official picnic sites. Never allow children to play with matches or throw cigarette ends away in the forest. If you see a fire in or near a forest, use the nearest telephone to inform the police or Forestry Department.

- **Do not frighten animals.** By making loud noises or trying to touch or photograph them, you may cause them to run in fear and be hurt.

- **Leave all gates just as you found them.** Although animals may not be in evidence, the gates do have a purpose; generally they keep grazing or herded sheep or goats in — or out of — an area.

- **Protect all wild and cultivated plants.** Leave them in place for others to enjoy. Flowers will die before you get them back to your hotel; fruit is obviously someone's livelihood. *Never walk over cultivated ground.*

- **Take all your litter away with you**.

- **Do not block roads or tracks.** Park where you will not inconvenience anyone or cause danger.

- **Walkers:** *do not take risks!* Don't attempt walks beyond your capacity. Remember that there is very little twilight on Cyprus … nor are there any officially-organised rescue services. If you were to injure yourself, it might be a very long time before you are found. **Do** *not* walk alone, and *always* tell a responsible person exactly where you are going and what time you plan to return. On any but a very short walk near villages, carry a mobile, whistle, torch, extra woollie, plenty of water, and high-energy food.

Wild boar are a rare sight — even more so than the elusive moufflon.

Touring

Driving on the roads of Cyprus (keep to the left) can be a great pleasure, but it does at times call for the ability to resist impatience. It can also be tiring in the hot sun. So do not aim for long distances. Better to really *enjoy* a shorter run than simply clock up kilometres. Punctuate days out in the car with short walks and relaxing picnics.

My touring notes are brief: they include little history or information that can be gleaned from standard guides or leaflets available free at all tourist centres and pavilions. Instead, I concentrate on the logistics of touring: road conditions, viewpoints, distances, and good places to rest. Most of all, I emphasise possibilities for **walking** and **picnicking** (the symbol *P* alerts you to a picnic spot: see pages 14-18). While some of the walk suggestions may not be suitable for a long car tour, you may discover a landscape you would like to explore at leisure another day.

The tours (which include 4WD suggestions — hiring a jeep is highly recommended) radiate from the three main tourist centres: Pafos, Lemesos and Larnaka. Bearing in mind that Cyprus is the third largest island in

VISITING NORTH CYPRUS

Pedestrians, cyclists and motor vehicles have been free to cross the 'green line' since 2003. It is a simple procedure, similar to any normal passport control. It is advisable to fill in the slip of paper available at the Turkish passport desk and have that stamped with the visa rather than have your passport stamped. The visa stamp (no charge) will allow you to spend up to 90 days in the north. Keep the slip of paper with your passport and have the visa cancelled on exit.

While it's *possible* to take a hire car to the north, most hire companies specifically preclude this or will not insure you. But it's very straightforward to take public transport to Lefkosia, cross the border on foot and hire a car on the other side.

At present there six active crossing checkpoints, shown on the touring map and the plan of Lefkosia with a red rectangle.

In and to the west of Lefkosia (Nicosia; Lefkoşa in Turkish)
Agios Dhometrios (Metahan in Turkish): Located west of the centre, this is the busiest crossing point — used by vehicles, pedestrians, cyclists, and goods hauliers.

he Mediterranean — some 222 kilometres (138 miles) from east to west — do not plan to tour the *entire* island without an overnight stop or two!

The large touring map is designed to be held out opposite the touring notes and contains all the information you will need outside the towns (town plans with exit routes keyed to the touring map are on pages 8 to 13).

Make sure your **car is in good condition**: keep a regular check on tyres, brakes, water, oil and lights. Always carry warm clothing (especially in the mountains, even in summer) in case of delays or breakdowns. Allow plenty of time for **stops**: my times include only short breaks at viewpoints labelled (🖼) in the touring notes. **Distances** quoted are *cumulative* kilometres from the starting point. A key to the **symbols** in the notes is on the touring map.

Some hints: All **motorways** (speed limit 100kph) are toll-free. Some **mountain roads** may be closed in winter. The **blood alcohol limit** is 50mg/100ml, lower than in the UK. **Telephones** (in green kiosks) are located in towns and most villages, near post offices, but most bars and cafes will allow you to make a local call if necessary. WCs are available in larger centres; others are found in bars and cafes.

All motorists should read the country code on page 19 and respect the environment.

Ledra Palace: Closer to the centre and used by cyclists and pedestrians — no motor traffic except diplomatic vehicles.
Ledra Street: Right in the centre of old Nicosia; for pedestrians only.
Zohdia (Güzelyurt in Turkish): Well to the west of Lefkosia, south of Morphou; a crossing point for vehicles, pedestrians, and goods.

British Eastern Sovereign Base Area (two crossing points)
Black Knight: At Agios Nikolaos, for vehicles, pedestrians, and goods.
Pergamos: This checkpoint, north of Pyla and Pergamos, is also for vehicles, pedestrians, and goods.

Whether you visit North Cyprus during your stay in the south or as a separate holiday, there's a superb selection of walks, restaurants and recipes in Walk & Eat North Cyprus *by Brian and Eileen Anderson (Sunflower Books)*

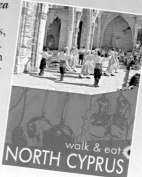

walk & eat
NORTH CYPRUS

Car tour 1: WESTERN WAYS

Pafos • Coral Bay • Pegia • Kathikas • Drousseia •
Prodhromi • Lakki • Baths of Aphrodite • (4WD
options) • Polis • Skoulli • Stroumbi • Pafos

*112km/70mi; about 3h30min driving; leave Pafos on the road to the Tomb
of the Kings (Exit D)*

On route: 🛏 at Smigies (4WD Route A); Picnics (see pages 14-18) 12,
13, 20, 22, (23); also 14 (4WD routes); Walks (11), 12, 13, 15, 19-22,
(23); also 14, 16 (4WD routes)

*A leisurely full-day tour on good roads which are narrow and twisting in places.
If you've hired a jeep for the first time, either of the suggestions on page 24
offers a good introduction to the joys of rough-track driving! Both 4WD routes
make shorter circuits than the full car tour — about 80km in each case.*

Leave Pafos on the road to the Tomb of the Kings (Exit
D), at the junction between Pafos and Kato Pafos.
At 10km pass a signposted turning to the right — a rough
track to the Mavrokolymbos Dam (*P*13); it's on the route
of Walk 13 from Kissonerga. At 11km reach **Coral Bay**★
(🔺✕🖎), the popular beach and resort area shown on
page 75, where Walk 13 ends. If you need petrol, head
about 1km or so towards Agios Georgios, where you will
find a station (🛢) on the right... and behind it, a reptile
display centre.

From Coral Bay, head inland to **Pegia** (15km ⛪✕🖎),
a large, cheerful, non-touristy village set on a hillside. As
you climb beyond it, the views (🖎) over the coast become
at first appealing and then magnificent as you head for
Kathikas (24km; *P*12), which means 'perched on a hill'.
Walk 12 sets off from the Laona Project Visitors' Centre
behind the church here, and if you find it open, there is
usually some interesting literature on display. The Laona
Project is a laudable attempt to breathe economic life back
into some of the old villages of western Cyprus, while
retaining their cultural and social identity.

If you drive through Kathikas and cross the main road,
you could detour a few kilometres to Pano and Kato
Akourdhalia, two adjoining, small Laona villages noted
for springtime almond blossom, a herb garden, folk
museum, excellent taverna/guest-house, and the 12th-
century church of Agia Paraskevi.

Our route bears left at the main road for a few minutes,
then turns left at a signpost through **Pano** and **Kato
Arodhes** (29km), **Inia** (31km) and the larger village of
Drousseia (33km 🔺✕🖎*P*22; Walk 15 and Alternative
walk 22), with its splendid views round the compass on
a clear day. Return to the main road, and turn left to
continue the tour — or first turn right briefly, then left

22

Farmer at Akoursos (Alternative walk 12 from Kathikas)

at a signpost to Kritou Terra, from where there is a short and very pretty walk to Terra and back (Walk 22; photographs page 97).

Continuing north from Drousseia on the main route, come to the coast road at **Prodhromi** and turn left to reach the fishing port and resort area of **Lakki** (47km ✕; photograph page 4). Just past the harbour, a fairly new development of luxurious blue and white houses, each one different and beautifully landscaped, catches the eye. Some 7km further on is the CTO restaurant at the **Baths of Aphrodite★** (❀✕▨P20), where Walks 19, 20 and both versions of Alternative walk 21 converge.

Returning on the same road, those with 4WD vehicles may choose one of the options described on the next page, via Neo Chorio, but if you are in a normal hire car you should come back through Lakki (61km) and Prodhromi to **Polis** (65km ▲✕▨🛈), an appealing town of ancient origin, and once centre of a thriving copper mining industry. From here follow the signposted main road (B7) back towards Pafos, with optional short stops and detours. At **Skoulli** (75km), the Herpetological Society of Cyprus operates the second reptile exhibition on this tour. You may not be fond of these creatures, but it's useful to know what they look like!

A right turn at about 83km offers a detour to Miliou (▲P23), a tiny Laona village noted for traditional weaving, and the start- and end-point for Walk 23. A few kilometres further on, a similar right turn (on an exceedingly narrow and winding road) leads to the totally abandoned village of Kato Theletra, where the threat of landslips led to mass evacuation some decades ago. It's an atmospheric place to explore (photographs page 99), but

4WD OPTIONS

After visiting the Baths of Aphrodite, head back towards Lakki, but make a right turn and drive 3km to the village of **Neo Chorio** (see reverse of touring map; normal hire cars can follow this stretch as well — even get as far as the Smigies picnic site, but will need to return the same way). Drive carefully through the narrow, winding streets, passing the church on your right, and emerge at the other side of the village. Beyond some water tanks on the left, the road reverts to track and forks…

Route A is signposted to **Smigies** — a concrete road leading in about 3km to the church of Agios Minas, from where it continues as a track to the well-equipped Smigies picnic site (⊐P21), where nature trails start and finish (see Walk 21). A well-shod hire car could make it this far but definitely *no further!*

Drive past the picnic site (on your right) and head for the T-junction on the skyline. Turn left, then, after about 150m, turn right in the direction of Koudounas (signposted). Keep going for just under 3km to another junction, where you again turn right towards Koudounas. This rough track (and it *is* rough!) winds westward toward the coast road which you reach some 6km beyond the T-junction at Smigies. The views are wonderful.

Turn left and drive about 7km to **Lara Beach** (*P*14; Walk 14; photographs above and pages 78, 79). The track is rutted, but gives access to a number of secluded beaches where you could skinny-dip with impunity, or picnic to your heart's content.

From Lara, continue on the unmade road past the signposted Viklari taverna on your left and the turn-off to the Avagas Gorge (Walk 16; photographs pages 80, 81). After 6km come into **Agios Georgios**, now on an asphalted road.

From Agios Georgios, where there is a small harbour, rock tombs and a church of 6th century origin, you have a simple drive of about 20km to **Pafos**, via Coral Bay and Kissonerga.

Route B follows Route A to the fork beyond **Neo Chorio**. Here turn left past a goat enclosure and drive for 5km to the once-Turkish village of **Androlikou**, which was abandoned during the Turkish occupation of the island in 1974. The village is now home to a single Cypriot family, a few sheep, a few pigs, a few noisy dogs … and around 1000 goats.

After you've inspected the old houses, taken some photos and assured the dogs that you're not Turkish, turn right for **Fasli** (another abandoned Turkish village). You soon come on to asphalt and pass the reason for the road surfacing — a new villa development with swimming pools in the middle of nowhere by the abandoned Turkish hamlet of **Pittokopos**. At a ridge 1km beyond Fasli, where a left turn would take you to Drousseia (see map pages 78-79), turn right along an appallingly rutted track for 1km, then turn left to gain wonderful views over the coast. This track takes you to the coast road, just above **Lara Beach**. From here the return to **Pafos** is as described in Route A.

24

Above: spring on the Agiasma nature trail at Kathikas (Walk and Picnic 12); right, from top to bottom: disused spring at Kato Arodhes; poppies and daisies; giant fennel (Ferula communis)

keep to the streets — the crumbling buildings could be unsafe. Old Theletra is the mid-point of Walk 23 — a superb hike.

As you pass through **Stroumbi** (95km ✕), keep a look-out on the left for the enchanting, colourful reliefs all along the roadside embankment. Some 6km further south, a right turn would take you to the monastery of Agios Neophytos (✝📷; Walk 11) — an optional detour of 8km return. From **Mesoyi** (105km), it's a short drive back to the centre of **Pafos** (112km), after a day spent exploring a varied and unhurried region of the island.

Car tour 2: OLD VILLAGES, ROCKS AND BONES!

Pafos • Geroskipou • Kouklia • Pano Arkhimandrita • Dhora • Arsos • Omodhos • Episkopi • Kourion • Petra tou Romiou • Pafos

130km/81mi; about 3h30min driving; Exit A from Pafos

On route: Picnic (see pages 14-18) (18a, 18b); Walks 17, (18)

A full day's tour, packed with variety and interesting scenery — mostly on good asphalted roads (but sometimes on terrible ones!)

Head out of Pafos on the Lemesos road (Exit A: Leophoros Yeoryiou Griva Dhiyeni). The first village, effectively a suburb of Pafos, is **Geroskipou** (3km ✝🏔✕🍴M), renowned for *loukoumi*, the delicacy shown opposite. Call it Turkish delight if you wish, but not within Greek earshot. One of only two surviving five-domed Byzantine churches on Cyprus stands here, Agia Paraskevi. (The other, at Peristerona, is visited on Car tour 5; see drawing on page 34). Also of interest is the Folk Art Museum: housed in an 18th-century building, it holds an impressive collection of implements both domestic and agricultural, plus rural apparel.

Pass the airport turn-off at **Timi** and, beyond **Mandria** (🍴), turn left to **Kouklia** (16km 🎫✕M), site of the Temple of Aphrodite and Ancient ('Palea') Pafos★. It is likely that old Pafos was destroyed by earthquakes in the 12th century BC, and there is little for the casual visitor to see, but the temple and nearby medieval manor are impressive.

Drive slowly through Kouklia. Then a tortuous road takes you to **Pano Arkhimandrita** (30km). Walk 17 (an all-time favourite with 'Landscapers') starts here, and it is worthwhile to pause for a short time to visit the shrine of Agii Pateres (see drawing on page 83) and view the scenery which is spectacular on all sides and brilliantly green in springtime (photograph pages 84-85).

The road continues on a rougher surface through tiny **Mousere** and skirts round **Dhora** (37km), to a junction (43km). Keep right, then go left at the next junction (44km), signposted to **Arsos** (48km), a village noted for its dark red wine. Drive in, if you wish, or just take the

Unusual sights always catch my eye. This 3m-high upright stone near Pakhna is pierced with a hole. A mystery. But one old Cyprus legend suggested that if a man could not crawl through such a gap, he had cuckold's horns!

26

Market stalls: loukoumi *(top);*
fruits and nuts

'bypass', eventually reaching a Y-fork signposted right to **Omodhos** (60km ♨⚔M). This larger village, too, is famed for the quality of its wine, and is well worth exploring. The pedestrianised central area is a touch commercial, but you have to buy your wine, *soujoukko, loukoumi,* lace, postcards, olive oil and terracotta pots somewhere, so why not here? Be sure to wander the narrow streets, too, and observe how exquisitely restored many of the houses are. The central Monastery of Stavros is modern but worth inspecting.

On the far side of Omodhos, turn left on a fast road (E601) signposted to Lemesos, passing turn-offs to Pakhna, Agios Amvrosios, Pano Kividhes and Kandou, before hitting the coast road beyond the A6 motorway and turning right to drive through **Episkopi** (83km ⚔🍴M). This is the centre of the British military presence on Cyprus, one of two Sovereign Base Areas — the other being at Dhekelia, east of Larnaka (Car tour 7).

Just beyond Episkopi is the ancient site of **Kourion★** (🏛⚔📷), one of the most important excavations on the island (open daily). Visit the tourist pavilion and acquire all the information you need to make the most of your visit to Kourion and the nearby **Temple of Apollo★** (🏛). Then continue east above Pissouri, from where you could make a detour to Alekhtora (*P*18a, 18b), either to picnic or to enjoy a short walk overlooking the Khapotami Gorge (Walk 18).

Our last visit for today is to the famed **Rocks of Aphrodite★** (103km ⚔). There is a tourist pavilion for your refreshment and enlightenment. It is said that the Goddess of Love was born from the sea foaming against the offshore rocks here (of which **Petra tou Romiou** is one; 'petra' means stone). From the rocks, Aphrodite was carried by a shell to the shore — a story most vividly illustrated in Botticelli's painting, *The Birth of Venus.*

Not far beyond Aphrodite's rocks is the Kouklia turn-off where we started up into the hills earlier in the day. From here it's a straight run back to **Pafos** (130km).

Car tour 3: LAND OF THE MOUFFLON

Pafos • Polemi • Kannaviou • Stavros tis Psokas • Dhodheka Anemi • Cedar Valley • Kykko Monastery • Panagia • Chrysorroyiatissa Monastery • Statos • Pafos

approximately 151km/94mi; about 4h driving; Exit B from Pafos

On route: ⏚ at Stavros Forestry Station, Cedar Valley; Picnic (see pages 14-18) 10; Walks 9, 10

A full day's tour, partly on narrow, rough and winding mountain tracks, best suited to 4WD vehicles, especially outside the dry months. The route is packed with variety and beautiful landscapes, so allow plenty of time. Those in standard hire cars can still enjoy much of the tour, by taking the alternative return route described on page 30.

Take Exit B from Pafos (Leophoros Evagora Pallikaridis). Some 13km out of town, turn right (signposted) to **Polemi** (16km 🖾), a large grape-packing community, and from here continue to **Kannaviou** (24km ✕).

Some 1.2km beyond Kannaviou, turn left on a dirt road towards 'Anadiou' and 'Sarama'. At the fork 1km uphill, go right for 'Stavros', now on an almost-level and well-graded, but narrow and winding mountain track. At 32km the interesting little church of Stavros tou Kratimaton (⛪) is signposted 300m off to the right — a pleasant picnic spot with benches. At 42km a track comes in from the right — from the Agia picnic site.

Stavros tis Psokas (45km ▲⏚) is named after a monastery originally sited here, called Stavros tis Psoras ('Cross of the Measles'; the spring at Stavros reputedly held holy water which cured that illness). The forests around Stavros are home to the timid moufflon, but you are more likely to see examples in captivity at the signposted enclosure here at the forest station.

From Stavros continue uphill, observing on the right the start of the Horteri nature trail (Walk 9), and come to a junction at **Selladi tou Stavrou** (small signpost). On the left is another short nature trail ('Moutti tou Stavrou', also described in Walk 9). Turn right here towards Kykko and come after about 8km to the **Dhodheka Anemi** junction (another tiny sign; 55km). Park here for a moment and consider walking the 4km to **Mount Tripylos** and back, to break up your day. The views from this peak (1362m/4470ft; *P*10) are magnificent. Walk 10 offers a long, but fairly easy circuit in this area.

The road straight ahead leads to Kykko Monastery after 17km, but it is more scenic to take the signposted road to the right — to **Cedar Valley**★ (65km ⏚), a lovely remote basin of tall, majestic cedars. This links up again

28

Top and left: Kykko Monastery is almost sumptuous in its decor, compared with more humble retreats. Above: the little church of Stavros tou Kratimaton on the track to Stavros is a pleasant place to stretch your legs

with the road from Dhodheka Anemi and then comes to a T-junction with the north/south running E912, where you turn right to **Kykko Monastery★** (84km 🅿🛖) — famed throughout the Greek Orthodox world and one of the biggest landowners on Cyprus. Kykko has an interesting history both ancient and recent; it contains, among other treasures, an icon attributed to St Luke.

Returning from Kykko, turn sharp right just past the tacky tourist kiosks, alongside the monastery wall. The road winds steeply uphill, past the ornate bell-tower shown overleaf, to **Throni★** (85.5km 📷), the mountain-top tomb of Archbishop Makarios, from where the views are superb. The archbishop can enjoy them now too: his 10-metre-high, 11 tonne bronze statue, which used to be Lefkosia's main tourist attraction, has been moved here — quite a feat, considering the mountain roads!

Bell-tower on the road to Throni

From Throni the main tour follows a *very* rough track. Head back through the one-way system at Kykko and turn right when you reach the main road.* At the next junction (having passed the kiosks again), turn left. Then, at the first left-hand hairpin bend, go straight across towards 'Mylikouri'. Immediately, turn right on a road signposted to the Vryssi Restaurant. After the restaurant the way becomes very rough and narrow. Follow this track for 16km — to the first fork, where you should turn right. Turn left after 5km at the next fork, and left again — to come to **Pano Panagia** (119km), the birthplace of Makarios, where you meet surfaced road.

Beyond Panagia, you have three options for your return to Pafos. You can continue on the good road through Asproyia to Kannaviou, from there retracing the outward journey. But you may wish to see **Chrysorro-yiatissa Monastery★** (🕯🛍📷), only 1.5km from Panagia. From the monastery head south to **Statos**, then *either* proceed via Pendalia and the E606 to the coast road and turn right; *or* head for the Pafos–Polis road via Khoulou, Letimbou and Tsadha. Each of the three options brings you back to **Pafos** after about 151km, rounding off a perhaps tiring but spectacular day in high and holy places.

* **Alternative return on asphalt roads:** If you are in a standard hire car, from Throni retrace your route back to **Stavros**. Then take the Lyso road (next to the café and forestry station). This good road winds through thickly forested slopes, with fine views to the mountains and a heady aroma of conifers. Ignore left turns to Sarama and Melandra. Beyond a monument to the EOKA fighters (121km), you come into **Lyso** (124km ✕), a lovely hilltop village with a cultural centre and several tavernas.

Take the road to Polis on leaving the village, passing **Meladeia** (🍴) before reaching beautifully kept **Peristerona** (126km **M** — not to be confused with the Peristerona near Lefkosia, which is visited on Car tour 5). Together with Lyso, this was a base for the EOKA. It is worth a stop to visit the Byzantine Museum and to view the **Atichoulli Gorge** on the right at the end of the village. Many caves where the fighters lived are visible in the rock face of the gorge, but these cliffs are now the nesting sites of raptors and smaller birds. On leaving Peristerona, look for a sharp left turn, signed 'Pafos' (127km), and follow this road (🍴) above the **Evretou Dam** to the main Polis/Pafos road (B7; 130km). Turn left for the trip back to Pafos (157km).

Car tour 4: FROM PAFOS TO PLATRES

Pafos • Asprokremnos Dam • Nikouklia • Phasoula • Agios Georgios • Kithasi • Kedhares • Agios Nikolaos • Pera Pedi • Saittas • Platres

approximately 67km/41mi; about 1h30min driving; Exit A from Pafos

On route: ⛨ around Troodos (see map pages 54-55); Picnics (see pages 14-18) 1-5, 8; Walks 1-6; 8

An easy but pretty drive from Pafos through a picturesque river valley into the Troodos foothills, where you can link up with Car tour 5 if you wish to continue to Lefkosia, and a choice of return routes to Pafos.

It's a lot easier that it once was to reach the Troodos Mountains from Pafos. There is still no *fast* way of doing it, but who wants one?

This is arguably the most direct route, and it is certainly a most attractive morning's drive. Leave Pafos at Exit A on the Lemesos road, and take the first major left turn after the airport turn-off. It is signposted to the **Asprokremnos Dam**, which is reached at about 14km. This is one of the larger (and newer) reservoirs on the island, and you should cross the dam wall very slowly, because the speed-reducing ramps are quite severe. Turn left on the far side and come to **Nikouklia**.

You are on the E616 in the beautiful Dhiarizos Valley, gloriously green in spring, when the river flows along nicely to your right (later in the year it may be bone dry). On the far side of the river is the abandoned Turkish village of Souskiou, with its old mosque, while a wind farm dominates the skyline. Beyond **Phasoula** (25km), with another poignant disused mosque next to a newish church, proceed very easily through **Agios Georgios**,

In the beautiful Dhiarizos Valley

Illuminated towers of the church at Pedoulas (Option 3 below)

Kithasi and **Kedhares** to **Agios Nikolaos** (44km) which offers a choice of tavernas and some lovely views westward over the upper valley.

After leaving Agios Nikolaos, the road narrows and you start to get impressive views of the Troodos Mountains. Continue to **Mandria**, then turn right to **Pera Pedi** (56km; *P*8 and Walk 8) and **Saittas** (✗*P*4). Turn left to **Platres**★ (67km 🏔✗🍴📷⊕). This mountain resort, with its pine-fresh air, has all the facilities you could want, and nearby are many walk options (*P*1-5; Walks 1-6; see area map pages on 54-55 and photographs on pages 51-61).

You can now follow Car tour 5 for a run of about 80km via Troodos to Lefkosia on good roads. But there are several appealing options for a return drive to Pafos.

Option 1: Follow the early section of Car tour 5 in reverse from Platres to Lemesos (about 40km), then it's another 72km along the coast road back to Pafos.

Option 2: Retrace your route as far as Mandria, then follow signs to Omodhos, from where you can drive part of Car tour 2 in reverse — via Mallia, Dhora, and Pano Arkhimandrita. When you reach the coast road at Kouklia, return to Pafos (about 130km in total).

Option 3: For a really full day's sightseeing, set off early from Pafos to Platres and Troodos, then drive via Prodhromos and Pedhoulas to Kykko Monastery and Stavros. To finish, follow the asphalt road return for Car tour 3 back to Pafos (see notes at the foot of page 30), making a splendid 'Grand Tour' of around 150km covering the west of the island.

Car tour 5: A CAPITAL CIRCUIT

Lemesos • Trimiklini • Platres • Troodos • Kakopetria • Galata • Peristerona • Lefkosia • (Stavrovouni
Monastery) • Lemesos

approximately 200km/125 mi; about 4-5h driving; Exit A from Lemesos

On route: ⏚ at Platania and Passia's Meadow (both north of Troodos
towards Kakopetria on the west side of the road), also Kornos Forestry
Station a few miles from Stavrovouni; Picnics (see pages 14-18) 1-5, (7,
8, 25a, 25b, 27); Walks 1-6, (7, 8, 24, 25, 27). (Walk 26 is also best
reached from Lemesos.)

*A long circuit with many optional detours. Quite easy to accomplish in one
day if you like driving, but impossible if you want to do a lot of exploring. It
makes an excellent two-day outing with an overnight stay in Lefkosia. All
roads are asphalted.*

Driving in Lemesos is not for the faint-hearted! The
town's traffic management leaves much to be
desired, and one should especially be wary of kamikaze
moped riders. But here is an escape from such urban
perils. Leave the bustling environs of Lemesos at the
Polemidhia roundabout (Exit A; junction with Makarios
Avenue) and follow the Platres and Troodos sign. This
road allows comparatively swift transit from the coast to
the mountains in barely an hour. Pass the Polemidia Dam
on your left after a few kilometres, then the Kouris Dam,
before reaching **Trimiklini** (30km ✖).

After Trimiklini, continue through **Saittas** (✖; easy
access to Walk 8 and *P*4, *P*8) and **Moniatis** before
coming into **Platres★** (37km ▲▲✖☎️🎦⊕). This resort
is fragmented around the pine-clad hillsides at an invigor-
ating altitude of 1100m/3600ft. Park awhile, and at least
explore the central area where you will find shops, banks
and a tourist information office. You may also care to look
at the Forest Park Hotel, where Daphne Du Maurier
wrote the novel *Rebecca*.

You might turn to pages 54-55 before resuming your
journey. It is obvious from this 1:50,000 scale map of the
Troodos region that Platres is an excellent centre for
walkers (especially those with a hire car), and there are
many hotels in the area, of all categories. Walk 3 finishes
in the centre near the tourist information office; Walk 6
is a short drive away.

From Platres the tour continues up to the trout farm
(**Psilon Dhendron**; *P*3, *P*5; Walks 3, 5) and **Troodos**
(45km ▲▲✖🎦). Do stop at the Forestry Department's
Visitors' Centre on the left (opening hours on page 49),
in order to make the most of the area. Troodos is a short
way southeast of Mount Olympus★ (🚻🎦*P*1), the

33

The church at Asinou, the finest Byzantine church on Cyprus, is open daily all year round and is a popular tourist attraction, particularly for Russian Orthodox visitors. Murals cover the interior.

Cyprus has hundreds of churches, ranging from tiny bare chapels in remote villages to ornately-decorated edifices containing priceless artefacts. You are likely to come upon long-ruined Byzantine churches with ages-old wall and ceiling paintings still visible. Many an old building is used by shepherds for shelter… for themselves or for their sheep and goats!

It is an unusual village that does not have a church of some kind. If the church is closed, and you would like to see inside it, ask at the local café, where they will readily raise the priest or caretaker, who will open the church for you. If you are exploring a place of worship, remember to dress in suitable clothing. It is also useful to carry a torch for the inspection of dark interiors.

Not every church is distinctive, but that of St Barnabas (Agii Varnava) at Peristerona, shown below, certainly is. Its five-domed structure dates back to the 10th century, and there is only one other five-domed church on Cyprus — at Geroskipou (Car tour 2).

There are mosques in Greek Cyprus, too, but almost all have remained closed since 1974 (a notable exception being Hala Sultan Tekke in Larnaka, of course: see Car tour 6 and photograph overleaf).

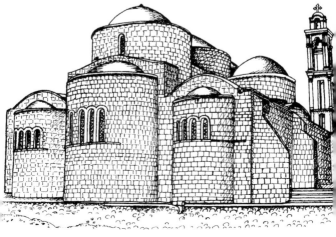

highest point on Cyprus (1952m/6400ft) and focal point for the island's short skiing season from January to March. Unfortunately, it's not worth driving to the summit — it's closed to visitors on account of its military radar installation and TV masts.

Walk 1 is a lovely way of experiencing Mount Olympus, although too long for a car touring day. But Walk 2 from Troodos is an easy leg-stretcher, with splendid views to the northeast (*P*2) and the route we are about to cover. The road sweeps past the Pano Amiandos mine on the right and the roads to Saittas (🚻 200m from the turn-off) and Kyperounda (*P*7; Walk 7). You pass two official picnic sites to the left and one to the right (🍴; *P*4; Walk 4) before coming into **Kakopetria** (60km 🚻🏨✕🚻 and 🚻 Agios Nikolaos 3km southwest) and **Galata** (64km 🚻🏨✕) — foothill villages which both reward exploration if you have the time, especially if you enjoy old churches.

This route (B9) goes straight to Peristerona, but consider first a 28km return detour to Asinou church★ (see panel opposite) from the Koutraphas crossroads, via Nikitari. Beyond **Peristerona** (85km 🚻), head straight for **Lefkosia**★ (117km 🚻🚻🏨✕🚻⊕ⅡM), the attractions, sights and peculiarities of which are fully detailed in tourist office material. If you are staying overnight, you might consider a brief crossing (on foot) into North Cyprus at the Ledra checkpoint (see pages 20-21), and you should certainly see the colourful Laiti Yitonia area near the city centre, the Venetian walls, the Cyprus Museum, and the ancient Cathedral of St John.

Leaving Lefkosia on Archbishop Makarios Avenue (Exit A on the town plan on pages 8-9), reach the A1 for a swift return to Lemesos in an hour or so. But a detour of about 18km return to Stavrovouni Monastery★ (*P*27 and Walk 27; Car tour 6; photograph page 111) is highly recommended. Other possible excursions off this route include the lace-making centre of Lefkara, but this could prove costly, as the good people of Lefkara will do their utmost to persuade you to spend! You may care to dally at Governor's Beach, still popular with British ex-pats and where there is a pleasant beachside café, or call at Agios Georgios Alamanou. Walk 24 starts at this distinctive blue and white monastery, shown on page 101. Beyond here you pass the road to Kellaki (photograph page 103), from where Walk 25 descends to the Germasogia Dam (photograph pages 106-107; *P*25a) just northeast of **Lemesos**, which you should reach after some 200km, *without detours*.

Car tour 6: THE HEIGHT OF ORTHODOXY

**Larnaka • Hala Sultan Tekke • Kiti • Dhromolaxia •
Kalokhorio • Pyrga • Stavrovouni Monastery •
Kophinou • Larnaka**

approximately 100km/62mi; about 3h driving; Exit B from Larnaka

On route: ⊓ at the Kornos Forestry Station a few miles from
Stavrovouni; Picnic (see pages 14-18) 27, 28; Walks 27, 28

*A full day out from Larnaka, taking in a Moslem holy place, one of the finest
churches on Cyprus and the pinnacle of Stavrovouni. All roads are asphalted.*
**Note: Women are not allowed to enter Stavrovouni, nor is photography
permitted.**

Take the road south to the airport (Exit B) for the start
of this compact tour, and notice the shimmering
whiteness of the Salt Lake, which is exploited commer-
cially in the summer months. In winter, if it rains and the
lake fills up, it becomes a refuge for thousands of
flamingoes and other migratory birds.

Just past the airport, turn right to palm-shrouded **Hala Sultan Tekke**★ (5km ⚓🏛✕), the third most important place of Moslem pilgrimage, after Mecca and Medina. It is a shrine revered as the burial place of the prophet Mohammed's aunt. Take off your shoes and go inside…

'Twas in the mid-7th century during an Arab raid on the island that Umm Haram, maternal aunt of the prophet, was travelling with her husband when she fell from her mule and broke her neck. She was buried at once 'in that fragrant spot'. The location, shown opposite, is indeed beautiful, with the mosque and its minaret surrounded by gardens and trees. It is as much frequented by tourists as pilgrims these days, and there is a restaurant nearby. Excavations to the west of the mosque have revealed the site of a Bronze Age town and many historically valuable artefacts.

After visiting the Tekke … put your shoes on again and return to the main road, turning right to reach **Kiti** village (11km ⚓✕), which is notable only for the church shown on page 114 — the magnificent Panagia Angeloktistos★ ('built by angels'). It houses the finest Byzantine mosaics on Cyprus. Walk 28, which takes in a Venetian watch-tower and another lovely church (photographs page 113) starts and ends nearby. If you've packed bathing things, you might like to try a short version of this hike (**P28**).

Come back on the same road as far as **Meneou**, then turn left to pass through **Dhromolaxia**, shortly reaching a crossroads, at which keep ahead to **Kalokhorio** (26km ⚓). Head for **Agia Anna**, then **Pyrga** (35km ⚓✕).

Some 1.5km beyond Pyrga you will meet the old Lefkosia/Lemesos road (⛱ near the Kornos Forestry Station). Turn left and after another 1.5km find the signposted turn-off left to Stavrovouni. The monastery is reached after an unprepossessing drive of 10km — past a quarry and an army camp (remember not to take photographs in this area). **Stavrovouni Monastery**★ (48km ⚓📷**P27**) is the goal of Walk 27. The approach is by way of a series of hairpin bends, but the road (once a rough track) is now asphalted. The views are astounding.

After your visit, follow the *old* Lemesos road south as far as **Kophinou** (70km ✕), and then turn left for a straight run back to **Larnaka** (about 100km).

Left: flamingoes at Hala Sultan Tekke's Salt Lake

Car tour 7: THE FAR EAST

Larnaka • Dhekelia crossroads • Phrenaros • Dherinia • Paralimni • Protaras • Cape Greco • Agia Napa • Xylophagou • Larnaka

100km/62mi; about 3h driving; Exit A from Larnaka

On route: ⊓ at Xylotimbou; Picnics (see pages 14-18) 29, 30; Walks 29, 30

A full day, offering a variety of popular beaches, quiet seaside picnic spots, country roads ... and a view to Famagusta in North Cyprus. All roads are asphalted; a few are narrow.

Hit the Dhekelia road north out of Larnaka (Makarios III; Exit A), first passing a light industrial area, with petroleum storage tanks much in evidence. But having left these behind, you are heading for the southeastern extremity of the island, which boasts the best beaches and accompanying crowds, but has a quiet charm, too. A wide variety of produce is grown in the rich red soil. Water is a precious commodity at the agricultural end of the island, and windmills abound, drawing water out of the ground to irrigate crops of potatoes and other vegetables.

As the industrial area ends, the beaches start, and to your right you will see a shoreline which is recreational for several kilometres, offering watersports, hotels, apartments and restaurants.

At the **Dhekelia crossroads** (14km) head north on the

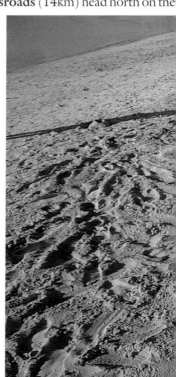

The hot Cyprus sun can do strange things to one's body. Here at Nissi Beach, as afternoon shadows lengthen, these sunseekers are oblivious to the way they look after hours of trying to achieve a golden-brown, all-over tan. Very easy to do at Nissi, but don't stay too long. Meanwhile, the fellow at the top obviously has a touch of sunstroke. He thinks he has scored with a beach beauty. But don't squeeze too hard, friend, or the lady will go to pieces...

E303, following signposting for Famagusta. You pass a turn-off for Pergamos (crossing point for North Cyprus; see pages 20-21). The road bends around Xylotimbou (⌂) and then Athna in North Cyprus. Our route passes through a corridor of the British Eastern Sovereign Base Area, leading almost to Agios Nikolaos (where there is another crossing point).

Turn right short of 'Aye Nick' (as the locals call it) and head for **Phrenaros** (38km) and from there to **Dherinia** (42km ✕), only a few kilometres from Famagusta in North Cyprus. In the opposite direction (our continuing route) lies the larger village of **Paralimni** (45km ▲✕🛒). Follow the signs for Protaras and Cape Greco for a few kilometres, almost on the coast, passing through an area noted for its forest of windmills — a vital part of the irrigation system in this agricultural region.

At **Protaras★** (57km ♦▲✕) there is an excellent beach and ancillary development which mushroomed in the early 1980s. Be sure not to miss the lovely church of Profitis Ilias (shown overleaf) while you're here. The whole area between Protaras (or 'Fig Tree Bay', as it is also called) and Agia Napa is splendid for picnicking and walking. Those who want a real constitutional can combine Walks 29 and 30. For suggestions, a large-scale

The modern church of Agios Elias at Protaras is most attractive. Many lovely old churches can be explored in this area — among them the little cave church of Agii Saranta, shown on page 120 (Picnic 30). Both Agios Elias and Agii Saranta are visited on Walk 30.

map, and more photographs of this area, see pages 115 to 120.

The road continues south, turns sharp right above Cape Greco and the Radio Monte Carlo transmitter masts, and continues to **Agia Napa★** (66km ♨ ▲ ✕ ⊕ ⊕ *P*29, *P*30), another much-developed tourist area, thanks to its fine beaches. At the centre of Agia Napa is an again-thriving monastery, used now as an ecumenical centre. Note the 600-year-old sycamore at its entrance.

The return to Larnaka passes the turn-off to Nissi Beach, heading then (partly on the A3 motorway) via **Xylophagou** (78km ✕), a market-gardening centre, and **Dhekelia** (86km) back to **Larnaka** (100km).

Walking

In this Seventh edition of the first-ever walkers' guide to Cyprus, I describe routes covering about 400 kilometres (250 miles) of the best rambling on the island.

The walks are designed to show you as painlessly as possible the wide variety of Cyprus landscape and to take you through a few communities not often troubled by the conventional tourist trade. In these villages, you will find the island at its most heartwarming. Here, a rambler with boots and rucksack might attract a few quizzical looks (Cypriots are strangers to walking for pleasure!), but the welcome will be genuine and hospitality generous to those who rest awhile.

I have indicated on the walking maps and in the notes where walks can be linked to create a more strenuous option, and any overlap or proximity of walks is easily seen on the fold-out touring map, where the walk areas are highlighted. But a word of caution: **never try to get from one walk to another on uncharted terrain**. Link walks only by following routes indicated in the walking notes or by following roads, tracks or specially designated nature trails. Do not try to cross rough country: this could be dangerous, or you might not have right of way.

Beginners: Many of the walks are easily accomplished by novices, providing you are sensibly shod and equipped. Check the short walk options and picnic suggestions for even easier rambles.

Experienced walkers: All the walks in the book should be within your stride, even the occasional bit of scrambling.

All walkers: Please follow the routes as described in the notes, and if you are at any stage uncertain of the way forward, go back to the last 'sure' point and think again. Do **not** try to continue a walk where bulldozers or natural damage such as a landslide — even on a well-maintained nature trail — has made the way impassable or dangerous.

Waymarking and maps

The authorities on Cyprus have gone to great lengths to **signpost** and **waymark** some 52 nature trails, all in a downloadable booklet, with maps: search 'Cyprus Department Forests Nature Trails'. Unfortunately waymarking is often lacking at junctions. Some of the trails are quite tough, others may be subject to landslides (see Walk 12 and the footnote on page 68 for Walk 9) and potentially hazardous.

For all the routes described in this book, the accompanying **maps** should suffice. Originally prepared with reference to maps published in 1960s and 70s by the Department of Lands and Surveys in Lefkosia and the British Ministry of Defence, they have been greatly updated over the years. Some excellent **printed maps** are available *free* from the Cyprus Tourism Organisation: at a scale of 1:50,000 (and with town plans at 1:10,000), these can be obtained from the CTO before you travel (log on to www.visitcyprus.com, then click 'About us' to find the nearest office). Otherwise, ask for them at the tourist offices in the main resorts on the island. At time of writing, these maps covered the Troodos Mountains, Larnaka area and town, Pafos area and town, Limassol area and town centre, Agia Napa area and centre, the Paralimni/Protaras area and Paralimni town, greater Lefkosia and centre.

Hints: If you are interested in the **long-distance E4** route across Cyprus (shown on our maps), there is a description of the various stages on the same CTO website, under 'Discover' ➤ Nature Routes' ➤ 'Hiking'. Finally, the same website has an excellent interactive map which can be viewed over satellite imagery.

Brief **nature trail guides** should also be available on the island: these usually contain very basic sketch maps of the trails, with general comments and numbered points of interest en route, but no walk *directions.*

Finally, **GPS tracks** for some of these walks are available free from our website: see the page for 'Cyprus'.

Where to stay

For purely a walking holiday on Cyprus, an obvious area to head for is the mountainous **Troodos region**. Its focal point is Mount Olympus, and within a 25km radius you have a wide choice of walking opportunities. I have described the more accessible routes. Platres, a hill resort with shops, restaurants, banks, hotels and apartments, is the most popular centre, but there are others — Troodos, Prodhromos, Pedhoulas and Kakopetria among them.

At www.visitcyprus.com there is a searchable database of places to stay. It covers accommodation from five-star luxury hotels to economical self-catering apartments.

There is **good coastal walking**, plus splendid beaches, around the Agia Napa/Protaras area on the southeastern corner of the island. To the southwest there is pleasant strolling around Pafos. Interesting walking excurions can be made from Larnaka (notably to Stavrovouni, but also out to the southeast). If you're based at Lemesos, the Troodos region is reached in under an hour by road.

But increasingly, walking enthusiasts are enjoying the **Akamas Peninsula** in the northwest corner of the island, an hour or less from Pafos. You will need your own transport to do this area justice, and I would recommend hiring a 4WD vehicle. The hills, valleys, gorges and wild coastline around places like Polis, Lakki, Drousseia, Kathikas and Lara are still completely unspoiled, with some excellent possibilities for rural accommodation.

Basic facilities may be available at some (but not all) of the island's **monasteries**, but bedding is *not* provided. No charge is made, but a donation on departure is appreciated. This privilege is really intended for Greek Orthodox pilgrims, and as a tourist, if you really want somewhere cheap to stay, it is more appropriate to seek out a room in a village. This is a great help to the fragile rural economy, and you will get a good deal and a cheap, authentic Cypriot meal.

Accommodation for a maximum of three nights is available at the **Stavros Forestry Station** (see page 67); book in advance (tel 26-332144 or 26-722338).

Goats on the Akamas uplands, in mist

A highly satisfying way of exploring Cyprus on foot for the first time would be to **combine a week in the Troodos with a week on the coast**. That way, you would have time for some of that sun, sand and brandy sour!

Weather

The Cyprus climate is splendidly Mediterranean, with constant sunshine during much of the year, and with rainfall being confined to a fairly short and predictable winter, when temperatures remain at a pleasurable level.

The walker probably experiences Cyprus at its climatic best between March and early summer, when the countryside is a blaze of floral colour and the sun hot, but not unbearably so. September and October are good walking months too.

The high Troodos region is cold in winter (and can be so beyond Easter), with snow usually allowing skiing for about eight weeks on the slopes of Mount Olympus. Summer temperatures here can be high, but they are usually a few refreshing degrees cooler than on the coast and consistently cooler than in Lefkosia, where the mercury can go above 38°C (100°F) for days on end!

Important: Anyone planning a walking trip early in the year should note that rainfall can turn dry tracts into streams and rivers. Moreover, there might still be snow in the mountains, making trail-finding impossible.

AVERAGE TEMPERATURES

Month	Average air temperature				Average sea temperature		%age of days with sun
	Min		Max				
	°C	°F	°C	°F	°C	°F	
Jan	8.9	47.9	18.3	65	16.5	61.4	57
Feb	9.4	49	19.4	66.9	16.9	62.4	63
Mar	10	50	20.6	69.1	17.3	63.2	67
Apr	12.2	53.9	22.8	73.1	18.6	65.5	71
May	15.6	60.1	27.2	81	21.1	69.9	79
Jun	18.3	65	30	85.9	24	75.3	87
Jul	22.8	73.1	35.6	96	26	79.4	90
Aug	22.8	73.1	35.6	96	27.8	81.9	88
Sep	18.3	65	32.2	90	27.6	80	88
Oct	17.2	63	27.8	82	25.1	77	80
Nov	12.2	53.9	23.9	75	21.9	71.4	71
Dec	8.3	46.9	17.2	66	18.9	66.4	59

What to take

If you are already on Cyprus when you find this book and do not have items like a rucksack or walking boots, you can still enjoy a number of the easier walks, or you can buy some equipment in one of the sports shops. Please do not attempt the longer or more difficult walks without the proper equipment. For each walk described, the absolute minimum equipment is given. Do adjust the equipment according to the season; for instance, take a long-sleeved shirt and long trousers, as well as a sunhat, in summer months, and a fleece and raingear on cooler days.

Where walking boots are prescribed, there is, unfortunately, no substitute. You will need to rely on their grip and ankle protection and, occasionally, their waterproof qualities. If you do wear shoes, make sure they have rubber soles, preferably of the Vibram or Skywalk variety. The often stony and dusty tracks of Cyprus can be unforgiving toward the improperly shod walker.

Please bear in mind that neither I nor Sunflower's researchers have done *all* the walks in this book under *all* weather conditions. We may not realise just how hot or how wet a walk can be, depending on the season.

Nevertheless, if you intend going to Cyprus properly kitted out, you may find the following checklist useful. I rely on your good judgment to modify your equipment according to circumstances and the season. It is always wise to seek out local advice about conditions before undertaking any walk, especially in the hills.

walking boots (which must be broken-in and comfortable)
waterproof gear (outside summer)
mobile phone (the **emergency number is 112**)
torch (if only for inspecting the darkened interiors of ruined churches!)
long-sleeved shirt (sun protection)
long trousers, tight at the ankles
trekking pole(s)
small/medium-sized rucksack
up-to-date transport timetables
safety pins, string, clips

lightweight jacket
knives and openers
first aid kit
plastic rainhat
plastic groundsheet
water bottle
extra pairs of socks
windcheat (zip opening)
warm fleece
sunhat, suncream
extra bootlaces
whistle, compass
telephone numbers of taxi operators

Walkers' checklist
The following cannot be stressed too often:
- **NEVER walk alone** — four is the best walking group.
- **If a walk becomes unsafe**, do not try to press ahead.
- **Do not overestimate your energy**. Your speed will be determined by the slowest walker in your group.
- **Transport connections** at the end of a walk are very important.

- **Proper shoes** or boots are vital.
- **Always take a sunhat** with you, and in summer a cover-up for your arms and legs as well.
- **Warm clothing** is needed in the mountains, especially in case you are delayed.
- **Mists** can fall suddenly in the mountains.
- **Always carry water and rations** on long walks.
- In spring, normally-dry **riverbeds may be flooded**.
- **Compass, whistle, torch, mobile phone** weigh little but could save your life.
- **A stout stick** (or trekking pole) is a help on rough terrain and to discourage the rare unfriendly dog.
- **Do not panic** in an emergency.
- **Re-read the important note** on page 2 and the guidelines on grade and equipment for each walk you do.

Nuisances

Thankfully there are few nuisances to worry about when walking on Cyprus, but goat enclosures are often guarded by noisy **dogs**. If dogs worry you, you might like to invest in a 'Dog Dazer' — an ultrasonic dog deterrent which persuades aggressive dogs to back off without harming the dogs. These devices are available on the web at reasonable prices.

It should be noted that poisonous **snakes** are indigenous to the island, along with non-venomous varieties (see page 6 under 'Books': *Nature of Cyprus*). The chances of an encounter are slim, as snakes are shy creatures. As a precaution, however, it is wise to check under rocks or logs (perhaps with your walking stick) before settling down for a picnic, especially if you are somewhere very hot, close to water. Examples of all Cyprus reptiles, including snakes, are on view at the Herpetological Society's snake centre at Skoulli (near Polis on the road to Pafos) and at a similar centre between Coral Bay and Agios Georgios (behind the petrol station).

Lizards of all shapes and sizes abound, but these are good fun!

Photography

Photography is forbidden in some sensitive areas (eg near military bases or the 'green line'), but warning signs make any restrictions clear. Some museums and churches do not allow photography … it is good manners to ask in any case.

Greek for walkers

In the major tourist areas you hardly need to know any Greek at all, but once you are out in the countryside, a few words of the language will be helpful, and people will be grateful for your attempts to communicate.

Here's one way to ask directions in Greek and understand the answers you get! First memorise the few 'key' questions given below. Then, always follow up your key question with a second question demanding a yes ('ne') or no ('ochi') answer. Greeks invariably raise their heads to say 'no', which looks to us like the beginning of a 'yes'!

Following are the two most likely situations in which you may have to use some Greek. The dots (…) show where you will fill in the name of your destination. I'd recommend that you purchase an inexpensive phrase book: many give easily understood pronunciation hints, as well as a selection of phrases.

ASKING THE WAY
Key questions

English	*Approximate Greek pronunciation*
Good day, greetings	**Hair**-i-tay
Hello, hi (informal)	**Yas**-sas (plural); **Yia**-soo (singular)
Please — where is	**Sas** pa-ra-ka-**loh** — **pou ee**-nay
the road that goes to …?	o **thro**-mo stoh …?
the footpath that goes to …?	ee mono-**pati** stoh …?
the bus stop?	ee **sta**-ssis?
Many thanks.	Eff-hah-ree-**stoh** po-**li**.

Secondary question leading to a yes/no answer

Is it	**Ee**-nay
here?/there?/straight ahead?/	e-**tho**?/eh-**kee**?/kat-eff-**thia**?/
behind?/to the right?/	**pee**-so?/thex-**ya**?/
to the left?/above?/below?	aris-teh-**rah**?/eh-**pano**?/**kah**-to?

ASKING A TAXI DRIVER TO TAKE YOU/COLLECT YOU

Please —	**Sas** pa-ra-ka-**loh** —
would you take us to …?	Tha **pah**-reh mas stoh … ?
Come and pick us up	**El**-la na mas -reh-teh
from … (place) at … (time)*	apo … stees …*

Point on your watch to the time you wish to be collected

Organisation of the walks

Each ramble in this book was chosen for its accessibility from one or more of the main tourist centres on Cyprus. Walks 1-8 are ideal for anyone staying in the **Troodos/Platres** area. Walks 9-10 are accessible too, but are set in mountainous country, remote from any major centres, and a considerable journey is necessary to reach them, wherever you are based. From **Pafos**, Walks 11-13 are nearest, but if you have a car consider too Walks 9 and

10, 17 and 18, and *all* walks west of the Polis road (B7)
From **Polis and Lakki**, Walks 15 and 19-23 are close at
hand, but Walks 9 and 10 and all routes north of Pafos
are easily reached by car. **Lemesos** is the recommended
base for Walks 24-26, but Walks 1-8 and 17 and 18 are
within reasonable driving distance. Walks 27 (Stavrovouni Monastery) and 28 are best approached from
Larnaka, but Walk 27 is worth some kind of excursion
from *wherever* you are staying! Walks 29 and 30 in the
Agia Napa region are also accessible from Larnaka.

I hope the book is set out so you can plan your walks
easily. You might begin by considering the fold-out map
inside the back cover. Here you can see at a glance the
overall terrain, the road network, and the location of all
the walks. Flipping through the book, you will also find
at least one photograph for each walk. Having selected a
potential excursion from the map and the photographs,
look over the planning information at the beginning of
the walk. Here you'll find distance/hours, grade, equipment, and how to get there and return (by public and
private transport). Wherever feasible, I have also suggested a short version of the walk, for those lacking in time
and/or ability.

When you are on the walk, you will find that the text
begins with an introduction to the overall landscape and
then quickly turns to a detailed description of the route
itself. The **large-scale maps** (all 1:50,000) have been
annotated to show key landmarks. Times are given for
reaching certain points on the walk. Giving times is always
tricky, because they depend on so many factors, but the
times I give are rather slower than my own walking time.
Note that they **do not include any stops**! Allow ample
time for photography and pottering about.

Below is a summary of the symbols used on the walking
maps:

▓▓▓	motorway	↔	spring, tank, etc	■	specified building
▬▬	trunk/other main road	♦♦	church.chapel	Å	transmitter mast
▬	secondary/minor road	†	shrine or cross	∩⌇	cave.windmill
▓	loose-surface road	⊞	cemetery	⚒ ☀	quarry, mine.mill
—	jeep track	⊼	picnic tables	▯ ▤	watchtower.stadium
– – – –	path, trail	🕮	best views	♟	fire-watch tower
²→	main walk	🚌	bus stop	🏠	forestry house
²→	alternative walk	🚗	car parking	⛩	ancient site
--------	other CTO trail	ⵜ	CTO signpost	P	picnic suggestion (see pages 14-18)
●▬◆▬●	E4 long-distance trail	ⵟ	military warning sign		
—400—	height (50 m intervals)	▮	castle, fort	📖	map continuation

Walk 1: ROUNDING MOUNT OLYMPUS

See map pages 54-55; see also photographs on pages 2 and 56
Distance: 14km/8.7mi; 4h

Grade: quite easy; gentle ups and downs between 1700m and 1750m

Equipment: walking boots or stout shoes, fleece, sunhat, water, picnic; waterproof in winter

How to get there and return: 🚗 to/from Troodos; park at the northern end of the main street, at the junction with the E910, opposite the Post Office (or park at the Visitors' Centre southwest of the main square, pick up a leaflet listing the trail points, and start there). Or 🚌 to/from Troodos (Timetables A7, A9 and B7). *Note:* The Visitors' Centre is usually open from 10.00 until 15.00 (16.00 in summer), but is closed on all bank holidays and on weekends from November until May.

Shorter walk: Troodos to Chromion (9km/5.6mi; 2h30min; easy). Follow the main walk to Chromion and arrange to be collected there.

Alternative walk: Artemis trail (7km/4.3mi; 2h; quite easy, with gentle ups and downs between 1800m and 1850m). 🚗 to the start of the nature trail, some 0.4km up the road to the Olympus summit.

There is a riding stable at Troodos, so the description of 'one horse town' is not entirely accurate. It nearly fits, but development has seen a Forestry Department Visitors' Centre replacing the open-air kebab houses with their squabbling owners. I miss them! Still, Troodos is neither a town nor a village, but a collection of shops, small hotels, cafés and souvenir stalls. It's a community that springs to life at weekends and in summer and is the centre of activity during Cyprus's short ski season. Four kilometres from Troodos by road is the highest point on the island — the summit of Mount Olympus (1952m/ 6400ft). Though romantically named, the 'top of Cyprus' serves a prosaic function as the site of a TV transmitter and radar base (the latter featuring an enormous 'golf ball' which is a distinctive landmark) and is, unfortunately, closed to visitors. So while I can no longer recommend a detour to the top of the island, this circuit remains one of my favourite walks in the Troodos region

Start the walk at an INFORMATION BOARD for the **Atalante nature trail**, opposite the stone-built POST OFFICE at the northern end of the main B9 road in **Troodos** (just south of the junction with the E910). If you have the CTO's trail leaflet, prepare to be educated as well as invigorated… At about **8min** the path curves round the back of the JUBILEE HOTEL, much favoured by skiers and walkers. The trail doubles back on itself at the head of a small 'gulch', which is a dry as a bone most of the year. Keep left at a fork (the right option leads to the Artemis trail — and is also our return route). As the trail contours at about 1750m, soon you can look south towards Platres

49

and beyond. At about **25min** a wide panorama opens up, with even the Salt Lake at Lemesos visible on a clear day.

At **45min** you reach a THREE-WAY SIGNPOST and an open area with picnic potential and striking views (Picnic 1). Ignore the wide track up to the right and follow the trail past a wooden bench. Near trail point No 25*, observe a stream of drinking water on the right (but it may be dry in summer). Follow the trail past a VIEWPOINT at No 31, and come at No 37 to the tunnel entrance to the HADJIPAVLOU CHROMIUM MINE, which was worked from the 1950s until 1982. Keep out, if you have any sense! But you'll find shade here for a refreshment stop. Come soon to a signpost and follow the 'CHROMION' path to the left.

Beyond a stand of junipers (*Juniperus foetidissima*), screech to a halt near trail point No 48 (**1h50min**), to observe to your left Prodhromos village and the distinctive, abandoned Berengaria Hotel. On the horizon you'll see Throni, the peak above Kykko Monastery where Archbishop Makarios is buried. At **2h05min** the way becomes a little scree-like for a short distance. A few minutes later, notice a small abandoned QUARRY to the right; then, further on, look up the hillside for a clear view of the Mount Olympus TV mast.

A stone building below on the road signals **Chromion**, the end of the nature trail (**2h30min**; *not signposted* as this edition went to press). Exit here the weary, the sun-struck and the tight of schedule. Onward the rest of us! Walk to the back of the stone building, where you can pick up a faint track. Follow this LINK TRAIL diagonally uphill for something over 100m/yds (two-three minutes), to reach the **Artemis trail**, where you turn left. The trail crosses the runs of TWO SKI-LIFTS and gains a little height. Soon after the second lift there are some striking views across to North Cyprus and west to the coast above Pafos.

At around **3h** you should reach the secondary road leading to the TOP OF **Mount Olympus**, opposite the INFORMATION BOARD marking the start of the Artemis trail (Alternative walk). I don't think it's worthwhile trudging up asphalt just to say I've been to the top, but should you choose this detour, allow 3km/1h return.

The Artemis trail is another, slightly shorter (7km) circuit of Mount Olympus, not vastly different from the one just completed, but higher and a touch more dramatic. Save this for another day, *or* combine the two trails for a good long ramble. For the main walk, start out along Artemis, but then take the first obvious track off left after trail point No 4 (*before* point No 5). Ignore a faint track off left after 350m/yds, but 150m further on, go left on a rocky track; it curves back north to rejoin the **Atalante trail** between points 9 and 10. Turn left again, and you should be back at **Troodos** at **4h** or sooner, after a splendid introduction to Mount Olympus. There are spectacular views at any time of year, with richly coloured flora in spring, and you will have barely climbed a hill all day.

Troodos in snow — very pretty, but make sure you don't try to follow any of the trails if the powder is still deep!

Walk 2: TROODOS • MAKRYA KONTARKA • TROODOS

See map pages 54-55; see photographs on pages 2 and 56

Distance: 6km/4mi; 1h40min   **Grade**: easy; almost level walking

Equipment: stout shoes or trainers, sunhat, water, picnic; fleece and waterproof in winter

How to get there and return: as Walk 1, page 49

Alternative walk: Troodos — Caledonian Falls — Platres (12km/7.4mi; 3h40min; fairly easy descent of 600m/1970ft). At the crossroads reached in 35min, turn right and follow an easy, rough forestry road for about 5km to Kryos Potamos (info board), where you can pick up Walk 3. Or link up with Walk 5; there are endless permutations!

This splendid, easy stroll packs a wide variety of scenery into a short distance. It's a lovely way of getting some Troodos air after a drive up from the coast.

Start at the ROUNDABOUT at the southern end of **Troodos**, where a minor road rises to the signposted POLICE STATION. Follow the road or the crazy-paving path below it up to the POLICE STATION, opposite which you fork left on the signposted **Persephone nature trail**.

In about **15min** you come to the particularly attractive stand of tall pine trees and cluster of benches shown on page 56 (Picnic 2). You don't need a rest yet, so keep going until you reach an obvious VIEWPOINT (**23min**), from where you can look back the way you have come and enjoy a fine view of Mount Olympus. Then look ahead: to the left you'll see the unmistakeable landmark of the Pano Amiandos asbestos mine, with the road to Kakopetria, Galata and Lefkosia just to its left. Should you travel that road during your stay, you will get an entirely different view of Pano Amiandos from the other side. It is a mighty excavation.

Take note of a '2KM' sign on the left and, 30m/yds further on, turn left on a track (**29min**). Then keep straight ahead at any minor track crossings. Soon you will reach a wide forestry track at a CROSSROADS (**35min**), where Psilon Dhendron is signposted to the right (Alternative walk). Keep ahead here, too, and in under **50min** you will be enjoying a spectacular panorama. This area, known as **Makrya Kontarka** (Picnic 2), is some 1680m/5510ft above sea level and affords breathtaking views of Pano Amiandos, Trimiklini and Saittas villages, the peaks of Kionia and Kakomallis ... not to mention Lemesos harbour and Salt Lake, plus countless village vineyards. Plenty of seats are provided, and it's an ideal place to settle down with a flask and sandwiches...

Return to **Troodos** the same way (**1h40min**).

Walk 3: TROODOS • CALEDONIAN FALLS • PLATRES

See map pages 54-55; see also photographs pages 2, 51, 56
Distance: 6km/3.7mi; 2h05min

Grade: quite easy descent of about 600m/1970ft, but beware of turned ankles where the stony path (which can be slippery) twists and turns.

Equipment: stout shoes, sunhat, water, picnic; fleece and waterproof in winter. In spring, be prepared to get your feet wet!

How to get there and return: as Walk 1, page 49 (by 🚗, park at the Visitors' Centre in Troodos). For the return, take a taxi from Platres back to Troodos for your car, otherwise 🚐 (Timetables A7, B7)

Alternative walks: 1) Begin on 'Persephone' (Alternative walk opposite); 2) See the map: climb back to Troodos with Walk 5 if you're fit!

The Caledonian nature trail itself is a mere 2km long. But the going requires some attention because of twists and turns in the path and stepping stones which criss-cross the stream many times on your way to the falls.

Start out at the VISITORS' CENTRE west of the main square in **Troodos**: from the car park, walk just a few paces left on the main road, then turn right down the quiet old zigzagging road signposted 'PLATRES OLD ROAD'. After about 2km (**30min**) you come to a CTO INFORMATION BOARD below the PRESIDENT'S SUMMER COTTAGE. Take the path to the right. Now stop and listen ... for if it's high summer you may be hearing your first babbling brook of the holiday. Many streams dry up in summer, but not the **Kryos Potamos** ('Cold River').

There are numerous stream crossings, and take care on the steep wooden steps (**45-50min**), especially in wet weather. Nimble walkers might reach the **Caledonian Falls** (Picnic 3) in **1h05min**. But those of us peering at all the points of interest on the nature trail — and the less fleet of foot — might take around **1h15min**. Stay on the downhill path below the falls, following the stream. Half an hour later, the aroma of grilled trout heralds the TROUT FARM and restaurant (**Psilon Dhendron; 1h 45min**). Cross the road and continue into **Platres** (**2h05min**).

Caledonian Falls (Picnic 3)

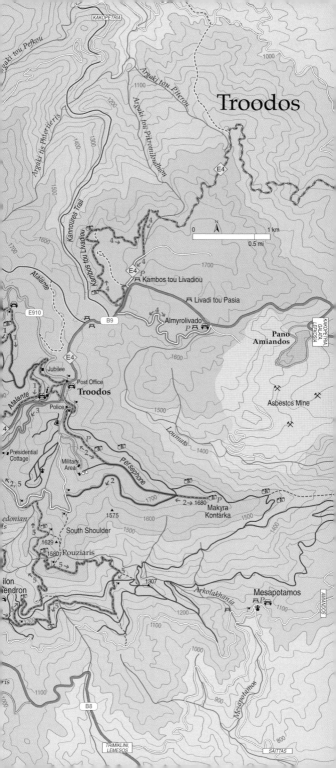

Walk 4: ALMYROLIVADO AND KAMBOS TOU LIVADIOU

See map pages 54-55; see also photographs pages 2, 51, 53, 56
Distance: 11km/6.8mi; just under 3h
Grade: quite easy walking at altitude on clearly defined roads and tracks with only moderate changes in gradient. Plenty of shade throughout.
Equipment: stout shoes, water, picnic; fleece and waterproof in winter
How to get there and return: 🚌 to the the Almyrolivado picnic site. From Troodos Square, take the B9 road towards Lefkosia for around 2.5km, to this picnic site on your right

This is a very pretty walk high up in the Troodos Mountains. You will walk in the shadow of Mount Olympos and enjoy some spectacular views across forested hillsides into steep ravines and to the north coast all without any real exertion!

Start the walk at the **Almyrolivado picnic site**: look for the old green road sign (set back from the site) which points toward Troodos and set off along this disused road. Notice the fenced area on your left: it's protecting some precious peat grassland, a rare habitat on the island. As you walk along this quiet old road, there are some good views early on across to the white 'golf balls' marking the Troodos summit. Look out for Bonelli's Eagles soaring high above you and imagine the days (not so long ago) when this narrow, winding — and occasionally precipitous — route was the only way to approach Troodos from Lefkosia. How times change!

When the old road rejoins the B9 (**38min**), turn right, passing a SPRING on your left after just over 100m/yds. A short way further on is the **Kambos tou Livadiou picnic site** with NATURE TRAILS (**43min**). Turn left into the site and walk a few metres up the asphalt road until you see two signposts, one pointing left to TRAILS 1 AND 2, the other straight on along the road to TRAIL 3. For the most part we'll follow TRAIL 2, so turn left here and head into the pines. You're now walking at an altitude of 1650m, 5400ft, not far below the island's high point of 1952m.

You pass strategically placed benches and a couple of wooden structures housing toilet facilities as the path initially winds around the southwestern contours of the mountain. After a few minutes you emerge from the pines — to a clear view of Mount Olympos to your left with the deep river valley plunging below you. As you continue along the marked trail, you'll pass the thick trunk of a PINE TREE (**1h10min**), still thriving but cleft in two by lightning strike — a dramatic foreground to more views of Mount Olympos.

The path winds round to the northern side of the

mountain, briefly passing an impressively steep drop falling away to your left (**1h20min**) ... before reaching a signposted VIEWPOINT with a wooden bench. Rest here awhile, to enjoy the breathtaking views down the valley to the spa town of Kakopetria and across to Morfou Bay and the Mediterranean beyond the island's north coast.

When you are ready to carry on, ignore the signs for Trail 3 heading back behind the bench into the pines and (with the viewpoint behind you, turning to your left) continue eastwards along TRAIL 2 as it contours around the mountainside. In a minute or two you will see a signpost indicating 'MNIMATA PISKOPON' (Piskopon footpath) and Kakopetria. This is your route.

You will head north, then east, through quiet, mixed pine forest where young cedars have been planted among the black pines to help with reforestation. There are a few small wooden boards with white arrows to help you along your way. Ignore a track to the right (**1h31min**). A few metres further on an E4 SIGN fixed to a tree together with a wooden bench in a large clearing confirms your route.

Come to a T-junction (**1h47min**): a LARGE WHITE SIGN FOR THE E4 long distance path points left to Kakopetria and right to Troodos. Turn right to join the main E4 back towards Troodos. Follow this signed forest track through the trees until it emerges on a small asphalt road, still the E4 (**1h59min**). Turn right here (don't go left — this is a restricted military area!) and walk briefly down the asphalt road. After about 10 minutes you will find yourself back at the start of the Kambos tou Livadiou nature trail board (**2h09min**).

From here just retrace your steps, crossing the B9 road and heading downhill for a few minutes before turning left and walking back along the old Troodos–Nicosia road. You should arrive back at the **Almyrolivado picnic site** in around **2h55min**. If you haven't yet had your picnic, you can head downhill for a few metres, to where there are plenty of benches and tables in the trees overlooking the grasslands.

Walk 5: PSILON DHENDRON • POUZIARIS • PSILON DHENDRON

See map pages 54-55; see also photographs pages 2, 51, 53, 56

Distance: 9km/5.6mi; 2h40min

Grade: moderate, with an ascent/descent of 400m/1300ft; good paths throughout

Equipment: stout shoes, sunhat, water, picnic; fleece and waterproof in winter. In spring, be prepared to get your feet wet!

How to get there and return: 🚗 to the car park for the Pouziaris nature trail at Psilon Dhendron (30m east of the car park for the Caledonian Falls), both just off the main B8 road. Or 🚌 to Platres (Timetables A7, B7) and walk to Psilon Dhendron

Alternative walk: Psilon Dhendron — Kryos Potamos — Caledonian Falls — Psilon Dhendron (10km/6.2mi; 2h55min; moderate, with an ascent/descent of about 400m/1300ft, sometimes on stony paths; access and equipment as main walk). Follow the main walk to the 50min-point. Take the path straight ahead and reach the rough forest road linking the Persephone trail to the Caledonian Falls trail (1h05min). Turn left and, from the Kryos Potamos shelter (1h20min), follow Walk 3 back to Psilon Dhendron (2h55min).

This is a wonderful circuit, with plenty to interest the nature lover and some marvellous views from the highest point. The ascent route follows an ancient mule trail, and the lovely woodland paths are full of bird life.

Start out by climbing the path to the left of the POUZIARIS NATURE TRAIL BOARD (just off the start of the signposted track to Mesapotamos). The path winds right and rises steadily through shady pines and junipers. As you bend left, notice the bench off to the right at a viewpoint (**6min**, Picnic 5) and a few strawberry trees, providing food for birds rather than for you! You'll see many more of them later in the walk. Cross a forestry road, going slightly left (**11min**). Five minutes later, turn left at a junction (**16min**); there is a sign here, 'PSILON DHENDRON 1KM'. (The path to the right is your return route). Now on a wide old MULE TRAIL, you enjoy magnificent views back over Lemesos and Platres.

Cross another forest road, again going slightly left at a HIKERS SIGN (**22min**), and eventually reach a welcome bench overlooking the Kryos Valley (**40min**). Round the slopes, with steep drops to the left, cross the bed of a stream (often dry) and after just 25m/yds turn right uphill on a path indicated by a sign fixed to a tree (**50min**). *(But for the Alternative walk take the path straight ahead.)*

The woodland path rises to the SUMMIT of **Pouziaris** (**1h 03min**) — not really a peak, just a plateau marked by a concrete slab. After taking in the superb views over the south coast from the bench here, continue a few steps to

On all your walks in the Troodos you will come across benches, ideally placed for contemplating nature: these are on the Persephone Trail. The giant 'golf ball' at the radar installation is a Troodos landmark. Bottom: the strawberry tree (Arbutus unedo) features prominently on this walk.

a junction (**1h05min**): Troodos is signposted as 6km, but you should head downhill, following the sign 'PSILON DHENDRON 6.5KM'. Your path now zigzags downhill with a few steep and stony sections. Descending through pines interspersed with more strawberry trees, you pass a bench (**1h 35min**).

Ten minutes later you cross a forestry road (**1h45min**). Go straight ahead on the signposted path — a rocky downhill stretch, followed by another sharp turn to the right and a long steady ascent. A large rockfall is easily negotiated and eventually you reach another welcome bench with views across the trees (**2h15min**). The path then winds to the right and descends quite sharply, to meet a track at the foot of a few steps (**2h23min**).

Cross the track, heading slightly right, and pick up your onward path. Continue down to meet the old MULE TRAIL coming in from the right (**2h26min**). Having rejoined your outgoing route, you'll soon hear the welcome sound of running water from the trout farm and come to **Psilon Dhendron** (**2h40min**).

Walk 6: TROODITISSA

See map pages 54-55

Distance: 11km/6.8mi; 2h55min

Grade: easy, with one uphill stretch of 2.5km (just over 150m/490ft)

Equipment: walking boots or stout shoes, sunhat, water, picnic; fleece and waterproof in winter

How to get there and return: 🚗 to Trooditissa, on the E804 northwest of Platres. Park 100m west of the entrance drive to the monastery, by a CTO signboard (or park in the monastery car park). Or 🚐 to Platres (Timetables A7, B7), then taxi to start and return.

Shorter walk: Trooditissa Monastery — Kambi tou Kaloyerou (6.5km/4mi; 1h40min; grade and access as above). Bus travellers could arrange for the Platres taxi driver to collect them at the Kambi tou Kaloyerou picnic site on the Prodhromos road (E804) — but they will not have escaped the climb!

Trooditissa Monastery, nestling in the Troodos Mountains some 5km northwest of Platres, was founded in 1250, and among its treasures are ancient icons and a leather belt decorated with silver medallions. Tradition has it that wearing the belt promotes fertility in women. Until a decade ago, one of the monks would happily produce this potent object for visitors, but perhaps because of increasing tourism, a large sign now proclaims that the monastery is not open to tourists — although if you are suitably attired you will have no problem visiting. In any case, this a very scenic walk in its own right.

Start at **Trooditissa**, about 100m west of the entrance drive to the monastery, where a signposted track, concreted initially, indicates 'AGIOS DHIMITRIOS 9KM'. (You could also use the path from the monastery car park to join this track.) The route soon curves round to the southwest, offering magnificent views over Phini village in the valley far below. When you reach another track leading off to the right (**20min**), ignore it for the moment — it's the return route. Continue down to the left, to a signpost indicating 'PHINI 4KM' (**25min**). Ignore this too!

At **50min**, at a clearing with a ROUND WATER TANK, a signpost indicates Agios Dhimitrios straight ahead, but we turn right, for a gentle climb of 2.5km to the Prodhromos road. This section of the walk is not in the 'brutal' category, but it can be a bit of a sweat in hot weather. Stop for a breather occasionally and puzzle over the inviting-looking tracks that lead downhill, but ignore them all. Keep on uphill to the TROODITISSA/PRODHROMOS ROAD (**1h40min**).

The **Kambi tou Kaloyerou** picnic site here is a pleasant location, with tables and benches among the tall

trees, barbecues and a play area for young children. This is an excellent place to take a break, or end the walk if you have arranged to be picked up.

Leaving the picnic site, head south along the road towards Trooditissa, and follow it for some 10 minutes, ignoring the first tracks off to the right. But when you come to a *sharp right bend* in the road (**1h50min**), take the track on the right (there should be a sign here, 'TROODITISSA 3KM', and you will spot a pair of CONCRETE WATER TANKS about 100m/yds away, in the woods). You now follow this track all the way back to the junction first encountered 20 minutes from the start. In its early stages, this track may be liberally strewn with rocks and boulders. The risk of further rockfall is greater after heavy rain, and it's possible that you will

have to return to the road and follow this to Trooditissa, should you be walking in winter or early spring.

The track is really a high-level version of the outward journey and offers spectacular views to the south and west. When you come back to the junction first passed at the 20min-point (**2h35min**), turn left, back to **Trooditissa** (**2h55min**).

61

Walk 7: MADHARI RIDGE

Distance: 7.5km/4.7mi, 2h30min; optional extra 3.5km (1h) round Mount Adelphi

Grade: moderate climb of under 300m/980ft; some short, steep stretches

Equipment: walking boots or stout shoes, sunhat, water, picnic; fleece and waterproof in winter

How to get there and return: 🚗 by car, leave Troodos on the Lefkosia road (B9). Beyond Pano Amiandos, turn off right for Kyperounda. After about 4km, turn left towards 'Spilia 5km'. Park 1.8km along, at Doxasi o Theos, where there is an information board on the right.

Alternative walks: The *approximate* routes of two other CTO nature trails are highlighted on the map below *in yellow*. Correspondents loved the circuit that leads from the starting point for the main walk north to Moutti tis Choras, then east to Selladi tou Karamanli, south to the foot of Adelphi and then down along the Madhari Ridge back to Doxasi o Theos. Total distance 13km/8mi; about 4h30min-5h, with climbs/descents of about 500m/1640ft overall. The other trail runs between two charming Byzantine churches — Stavros tou Agiasmati (a detour off the Peristerona road) and Panagia tou Araka near Lagoudhera. This out-and-back walk is 15km/9.3mi; 5h, with ascents of 600m/2000ft. To halve the distance/ascent, leave your car in Lagoudhera. You should be able to call a taxi from one of the coffee houses, to take you to Stavros tou Agiasmati. Walk from there back to your car.

Mount Adelphi is the second highest point on Cyprus (1613m/5290ft), and this walk to it along an exposed ridge is even more spectacular than the approach to Mount Olympus. It can be strenuous for short

stretches, and the track stony, but the views are stunning — from the northern, Turkish side of the island to the south, where Kyperounda clings to the opposite hillside like magic.

Start out at the INFORMATION BOARD for the **Doxasi o Theos** ('Glory to God') nature trail: climb sharply to the right and, when you come to a fork where you can go ahead or left, keep left. You soon reach a rocky outcrop with a wonderful view northwards towards Morphou Bay. At around **15min** come to one of several well-placed benches (Picnic 7) from where there are equally breathtaking views over Kyperounda and towards the Pano Amiandos mine and the 'golf ball' on Olympus.

Walk the trail through pine trees, and at around **40min** drop down to a small clearing with views over the Mesaoria Plain and towards Mount Adelphi — another setting for Picnic 7. This could mark the end of a short version of this walk if you didn't fancy the climb ahead. But it isn't as bad as it looks, honestly! It can be quite cool and breezy on top, even in summer.

Skip up to the TOP OF **Madhari Ridge** (**50min**) like a moufflon, and you'll be rewarded with wonderful views! You'll see Kyperounda again to your right, and Chandria with its striking modern church. Reservoirs

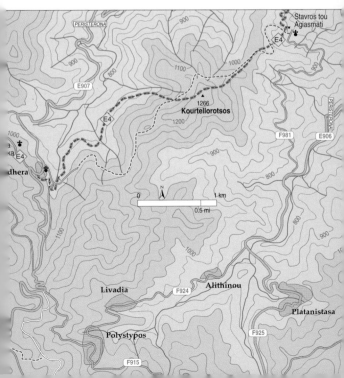

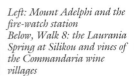

glimmer between the two villages. White cairns indicate viewpoints to your left (you climb slightly to reach them), then the FIREWATCH POINT at the peak comes into view. From the CTO board below the peak, climb the last stretch to the SUMMIT OF **Mount Adelphi** (**1h20min**) for some truly magnificent views — and, if you wish, do the extra signposted 'Teisia tis Madaris' circuit (add one hour). The fire-watcher usually has a three-day shift up here — rather a lonely existence. If he isn't busy, he'll be very happy to spend some time with you.

Then retrace your steps to the **Doxasi o Theos** INFORMATION BOARD (**2h30min**). If you haven't been impressed by the views from the ridge, the brandy sours are on me if we ever meet!

Walk 8: PERA PEDI • AGIA MAVRI • SILIKOU • KOUKA • PERA PEDI

Distance: 10km/6.2mi; 2h40min **See photos opposite (below)**

Grade: fairly easy, with an ascent/descent of about 300m/1000ft; all on country roads and lanes; *very little shade*

Equipment: stout shoes or trainers, sunhat, water, optional picnic

How to get there and return: 🚗 to Pera Pedi (the 56km-point in Car tour 4). Park in the car park and make your way to Neromylos Village Inn on the main street. Or 🚌 to Platres (Timetables A7, B7) and taxi

Short walk: Agia Mavri (6.1km/3.8mi; 1h40min; access, equipment, grade as above (ascents/descents of about 180m/600ft). Follow the main walk for 1h, then turn left to the E802 and left again, back to your car.

Alternative walk: Extension to Lofou (16.6km/10.3mi; 4h40min; access/equipment as above; moderate but long (ascents/descents of about 400m/1300ft). Follow the main walk to the 1h-point, then turn right at the crossroads. Entering Lofou, make your way to the main church. With your back to its blue gates, walk down a cobbled alley to the left of a lamppost. After about 100m turn left at a hiking sign for 'Y Vrisi' nature trail. At the end of the trail, head northeast to Silikou and rejoin the main walk at the 1h25min-point, then follow it to the end.

The five villages visited on this walk are very different, and all are delightful. Their livelihood comes from the vineyards you pass en route and, if you have time, you can visit a wine museum and sample the produce in a local taverna. Although the walk follows country roads all the

way, they are usually very quiet. (But bear in mind that they are busier at weekends when the town dwellers head out to the villages to visit family or tend their vines.)

Start the walk at the NEROMYLOS VILLAGE INN. Opposite, just to the left, is a crazy-paved pedestrian lane. Follow it over a bridge across the permanently running **Kryos River** (**1min**; Picnic 8). Ignore a fork to the right and turn left at the T-junction with a very old CHURCH (**5min**). Follow this lane as it bends down to recross the river and rises to the road to Agia Mavri and Vouni (**10min**), where you turn right. The road runs alongside the river and through the gorge. At the Y-fork just outside **Agia Mavri** (**25min**), you will turn left. But first have a look at this hamlet with its restaurants and little church.

Back at the Y-fork, now turn right (it should be sign-posted to Silikou). Follow the road in a deep U-bend to the right, then a sharp U-bend to the left. Two kilometres from Agia Mavri, go straight over a crossroads (**1h**). *(The Short walk turns left here.)* The road now descends past lovely vineyards to **Silikou** (**1h25min**) — one of the 'Commandaria' wine villages (producing dessert wines for over 1000 years), where there is a small WINE MUSEUM. Next to the village CHURCH you can see the LAURANIA SPRING, is set into the trunk of an ancient olive tree.

From Silikou head uphill towards Kouka and Pera Pedi. As you leave the village you will see a rather sadly neglected TURKISH CEMETERY on your left. Continue up to **Kouka** (**2h15min**), another pretty little village. As you walk through the village you will see a taverna on your left where you can pause for a pint of real ale from Cyprus' APHRODITE'S ROCK BREWERY. Next door is the church of **Timios Stavros** (Holy Cross. Just a few steps past the church take the left turning which leads uphill. The asphalt road runs out after a couple of minutes and you continue your walk along a loose earth track through some pine woods to the church of **Ag Paraskevi**.

Continue past the church on PARAMBALOU STREET, to the junction with the MAIN E802 ROAD TO PERA PEDI (**2h 30min**). Turn left for a couple of minutes, to where a left turn is signposted 'LOFOU 7KM'. Take a look at the SHRINE TO AG FANEROMENIS which is almost opposite this junction. The wax effigies of various body parts here are a rather strange sight to British eyes, but are common-place in Cyprus' churches, where people leave these votive offerings when they pray for a cure for whatever ails them.

Then continue ahead to **Pera Pedi** (**2h40min**).

Walk 9: STAVROS TIS PSOKAS

Distance: 14.5km/9mi; 4h20min

Grade: fairly strenuous, with ascents of about 550m/1800ft overall; some gravelly surfaces underfoot

Equipment: stout shoes or walking boots, sunhat, water, picnic; fleece and waterproof in winter. Trekking poles are useful for the gravelly descents.

How to get there and return: 🚗 by car from Pafos via Kannaviou, then track; from Polis via Lyso; from Troodos via Kykko Monastery. *NB: In winter and early spring, access from*

Forestry station at Stavros

Pafos via Kannaviou and track may only be possible in a 4WD vehicle, otherwise take the E702 via Panagia and Dhodheka Anemi. Park just over 1km outside Stavros on the Kykko road, by the Horteri nature trail information board (on the right). Or park at Stavros and start there.

Short walks

1 **Horteri nature trail** (5km/3mi, 1h30min; moderate-strenuous, with an initial ascent of about 250m/820ft) and a steep descent. Park at the nature trail board and follow the main walk for 1h30min.

2 **Moutti tou Stavrou nature trail** (2.5km/1.6mi; 45min; easy). Park at Selladi tou Stavrou junction north of the Horteri trail, where there is another nature trail information board. Follow the waymarked trail, walking in the *opposite direction* to the main walk (see purple arrows on the map). After 500m, at a junction, keep right (the path to the left, originally the route of the main walk, is no longer viable).

The Forestry Department runs a forest station at Stavros, where there is also a small café and very popular hostel accommodation (see page 44). To encourage intimate acquaintance with the environment, the department has also created two nearby nature trails, and information about the area is available from the forestry office. Take time, too, to visit the moufflon enclosure just north of the forestry office on the road to Lyso. This rare Cyprus sheep — which was once almost extinct —is a very shy creature, so chances of spotting it in the wild are rare! Since the Stavros nature trails are not adjacent, my 'grand tour' includes stretches of road-walking and could be quite tiring on a warm day. A much easier option is to do the two Short walks as separate circuits.

Begin at the **Horteri trail** SHELTER/INFORMATION BOARD (by a SPRING). Keep ahead at a fork two minutes up (you will return on the path to the left). The path rises gently but steadily through strongly scented pines. Excellent views over the whole valley setting of Stavros and to the fire-watch point on Horteri are your reward for reaching trail point No 16. Continue uphill to a fork

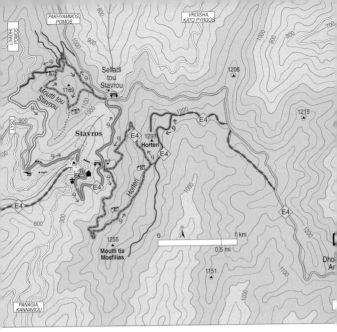

and benches at point No 22 (**50min**), where you keep left on the nature trail. (Heading right you could climb to the top of Horteri for even wider-ranging views over the Akamas Peninsula; allow 45 minutes extra for this diversion.) After a fairly steep descent, the trail descends to the HORTERI TRAIL SHELTER (**1h30min**).

From here follow the asphalt road north, to the **Selladi tou Stavrou** junction (**2h10min**). ('Softies' can drive here, to park for Short walk 2.) Climb the steps up to the nature trail and walk ahead to a fork, where you keep right, to *follow the nature trail in reverse* (but for Short walk 2 go *left* here). Soon, from a plateau, there is a fine view reaching west to the Akamas Peninsula. After about 1km you come to a track, where the nature trail path joins sharply from the left (almost back the way you came). *D* not follow this*, but turn sharp left on the *track*. Now jus keep heading south on tracks, then the earthen road keeping left at every junction. From time to time you will enjoy some good views of the Stavros valley.

The earthen road eventually descends to the Lyso road opposite a HELIPAD (**3h30min**), where you turn left t **Stavros** (**3h45min**). From here walk up the Kykko road back to your car at the **Horteri trail** (**4h20min**).

*There was a third nature trail which initially followed this path, the headed south down the ridge to the helipad. This prettier and mor direct route is no longer viable — presumably there was a landslide.

Walk 10: CEDAR VALLEY AND MOUNT TRIPYLOS

Distance: 14km/8.7mi, 4h

Grade: quite easy, with an ascent of about 250m/820ft; *but note that almost two-thirds of the walk is on road*. If possible, set out early; there may be heavy traffic in Cedar Valley en route to the picnic area or Kykko.

Equipment: stout shoes, sunhat, water, picnic; fleece and waterproof in winter

How to get there and return: 🚌 by car from Troodos via Kykko Monastery, from Pafos via Kannaviou and Pano Panagia, or from from Polis via Lyso and Stavros. Park 8km southeast of Stavros at the junction of the Cedar Valley/Panagia and Kykko roads; there is a road sign here, 'Cedar Valley 8km'. This area is known as Dhodheka Anemi (identified by a tiny brown sign on the Cedar Valley road).

Short walk: Mount Tripylos (5km/3mi; 1h40min; grade as above). At the junction you will see a track (barred to motor vehicles) signposted to Tripylos (if the sign is missing, look for E4 arrows). Park here and simply follow the track uphill for 2.5km; return the same way. (You can also approach from Cedar Valley: see Picnic 10 on page 16.)

Whether you make this walk your prime target for the day, or choose the shorter version while on a trip to Kykko, you are sure to enjoy it! The views are splendid, and the surroundings beautiful. The main (longer) walk will be a disappointment to many, as the loop road into Cedar Valley has been asphalted. But if you'd walked it in the past, swallowing the dust thrown up by 4WD safaris, you'd find it a great improvement … especially out of season or early in the day, when there's little traffic.

Begin at the **Dhodheka Anemi** JUNCTION: follow the road signposted 'Cedar Valley 8km'. This spectacular road

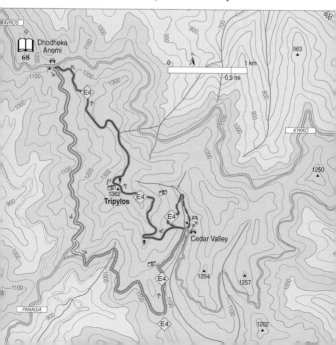

The forests around Stavros and Cedar Valley are in a healthier state now than they were in the early 1900s, and Winston Churchill can be credited for improving matters after 1907 when, as Under Secretary of State for the Colonies, he allocated funds for extensive tree-planting. The forests flourished in the ensuing years, but their welfare was not aided by the invading Turkish forces: in 1974 their air force needlessly set fire to over 150 square kilometres of trees. Recovery is continuing, thanks to the work of the Forestry Department.

makes a beautiful, easy-surfaced walk, gently downwards at this stage, through fragrant pine woods.

Some 3.4km along, where the road curves left, take the track off to the left (if you miss it, go left on the road 500m/yds further on.) Now you will experience stunning views to the south and west as your way curves gradually round to the east. After about **2h**, cedars will appear among the pine trees and become much more evident as you reach the area that gave rise to the name of **Cedar Valley**. You will come to a small PICNIC AREA with a water supply, close to a group of plane trees (**2h30min**).

Just west of the picnic area, take the E4 track that first heads west, then dips south in a large hairpin. (Ignore the diversion off to the right after 200m/yds — it's just a loop round the picnic area.) The track then heads north, and views open out all around. It's a gentle climb of 2km, and you may be lucky enough to spot a moufflon in the wild. Cedar trees are still very much in evidence as you approach the SUMMIT OF **Mount Tripylos** (**3h30min**). From this peak (1362m/4470ft) there are magnificent views — eastward to Troodos, westward to the Akamas, and north to Morphou Bay. At the top there's a fire-watch station and a lovely small picnic area (Picnic 10).

From here it's a simple stroll of 2.5km back to **Dhodheka Anemi** and your car, reached in around **4h**. On a clear day the air could not have been fresher, nor the views more appealing.

70

Walk 11: CIRCUIT FROM AGIOS NEOPHYTOS

Distance: 6.5km/4mi, 1h50min

Grade: moderate; steep initial ascent and steep final descent on a rough, (seasonally) overgrown path. Ascent/descent about 250m/820ft overall

Equipment: walking boots or stout shoes, sunhat, water, long trousers; optional trekking pole(s)

How to get there and return: 🚗 car or taxi to/from Agios Neophytos. Or 🚌 from Pafos (Timetable E9); return on the same bus from Tala (2km away). Or Pafos-Polis 🚌 (Timetable E5) to Tsadha, then 1km on foot: join the walk at the 1h-point and circle back to the same point.

The 12th-century monastery of St Neophytos is about 10km north of Pafos and dedicated to a man who was a noted scholar and writer, devoted man of God, and a hermit who chose a life of reclusion in caves that can still be seen by visitors. Some have beautiful frescoes that can be closely inspected, whether on a car outing or as a prelude to this circuit of the monastery valley.

Start out at **Agios Neophytos** by walking back towards Pafos and *past* the turning for Tala. Just 80m/yds past the Tala turn-off (80m *before* an old stone warehouse with recent extension), turn sharp left up a track. This rises fairly steeply (**5min**), but the effort is rewarded with ever-improving views over the monastery. Ignore a track off left and a grassy track right, then turn sharp left and either round three sides of an OLIVE GROVE or cut 60m straight across it — to a road (**15min**). Turn left uphill. When the road ends abruptly, climb a low bank, join another track and head up towards two houses. Meet another road and follow it left, past these houses, for 40m/yds, then head left on a track below the summit of **Melissovounos**. Ignoring a track off left, continue steadily uphill towards the radio aerials. (If you wish, take a detour of 300m/yds to the top, to gain views towards Pafos and the coast.)

Otherwise, turn sharp left and follow the track uphill to the CREST (**45min**), from where it gently undulates.

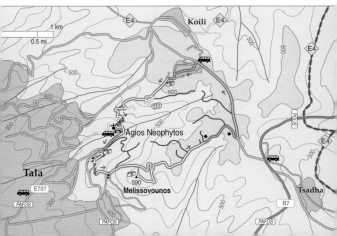

As you rise at the start of the walk, there are fine views back to Agios Neophytos. Left: wall painting at the monastery

Ignore any turn-offs. The track, now tarmac, passes some houses and meets a quiet road (**1h**) where you turn left. After about 1km, just past a bus shelter on the right, turn left on ARCHIP MAKARIOU III through a housing estate in **Koili**. Ignore a first street off right; after about 100m/yds the street you are on bears right. At a T-junction, go left, then turn right on MAKADONIAS STREET. After 30m turn left downhill on a concrete track through vineyards (**1h20min**), with splendid views towards the distant coast and the masts on Melissovounos ahead. Keep to the main track; as it bears slightly right, ignore a track to the left. You are walking past a vineyard on your left; at the end of the vines your track turns sharply left — to a junction of four tracks. Take the first track to the right. You will soon see the Tala road across the valley to your right.

As your route turns 90° left, ignore a rocky path to the right. About 70m further on, leave the main track and turn sharp right (just before a left-hand bend) onto a downhill track (**1h30min**). Some 300m/yds down this track, on a narrow hairpin bend to the right, walk left for about 20m/yds, to where the main, rocky path to the monastery zigzags down left. It's obvious in summer, but may be overgrown in winter and spring. At time of writing an arrow of loose stones on the ground pointed to the path. Follow this down to the large WATER TANK at **Agios Neophytos** (**1h50min**).

Walk 12: AROUND KATHIKAS

See photograph page 25   **Distance**: 7.5km/4.7mi; 1h50min

Grade: easy (ascents/descents 100m/300ft), *but the nature trail is subject to mud slides, and the walk should be avoided during or following wet weather.*

Equipment: walking boots or stout shoes, sunhat, water, picnic

How to get there and return: 🚗 car to/from Kathikas

Short walk: Agiasma nature trail (3.5km/2.2mi; 1h; easy). Follow the main walk for 45min, then turn left to Kathikas.

Alternative walk: Akoursos (11km/6.8mi; 3h; easy, but with a return climb of 280m/920ft. At the 1h08min-point detour to Akoursos, an old village with a disused mosque, old olive press ... and spooky cemetery.

This walk, in an area developed by the Laona Project (see page 22) gives stunning views down a ravine full of jackdaws to the coast at Coral Bay. We then walk through vineyards, flushing partridge by the score.

Start from the CHURCH in **Kathikas**. Walk south on the signposted Akoursos road and after 250m/yds turn right on AGIASMATOS STREET, which soon bears left. After 800m, turn right on the signposted **Agiasma nature trail** (**15min**). The rocky path descends past a turning to the 'official' start of the trail and comes to a bench at a SPRING (**20min**; Picnic 12; photo page 25). Take the path to the right, cross the ravine and ascend under the cliffs, before contouring along the edge for a short way. Turn left on a track and at the next sign turn left and zigzag up to another bench (**39min**), with a fine view to distant Coral Bay.

Continue to a dirt road and turn left to a crossroads (**45min**). Turn right *(left for the Short walk)*, pass the chapel of **Agia Marina**, then stroll on to a T-junction with a concrete road (**1h10min**). Turn left and in five minutes cross the Akoursos road (or first detour right; *Alternative walk*). Go straight over a crossing track 400m further on. After another 600m *turn sharp left* off the main track on a lesser track edging a vineyard (*easily missed!*: it's 100m *before* a stronger track to the left which passes a small house). Two minutes later go straight over a crossroads. In another two minutes go right at a Y-fork and ignore a sharp turn to the right. Some 250m further turn left. Ignore any tracks right or left until you reach a T-junction (**1h 35min**), where you turn right. After 200m turn left on a clear track; this bears left to the road (**1h40min**), where you turn right to **Kathikas** (**1h50min**).

Walk 13: KISSONERGA TO CORAL BAY

Distance: 9.5km/6mi, 2h45min
Grade: easy, ascents of only 100m/330ft
Equipment: stout shoes, sunhat, water, picnic, swimming things
How to get there: 🚗 car or taxi to Kissonerga; by car park near the sports ground near the church. (Travelling by taxi, you could start at the 30min-point, to avoid road-walking.) Or 🚌 from Pafos (Timetable E7); alight at the sports ground
To return: 🚌 from Coral Bay to Pafos (Timetable E8), or to the junction of the Coral Bay/Kissonerga road, from where it is a 15min walk back to your car. Some buses return from Coral Bay to Pafos via Kissonerga (check at the tourist office or with Pafos Transport: see Timetable E8).

A few decades ago this ramble to the main irrigation reservoir of the Pafos region was marred by the intrusion of a military camp. But because it is so close to Pafos and so easy, it remains popular with 'Landscapers'.

The walk starts at **Kissonerga**, a village straddling the road between Pafos centre and Coral Bay. From the southern end of the SPORTS PITCH by the BUS STOP, walk north for 50m/yds or so, then turn right up APIS STREET (just before the PRIMARY SCHOOL on the right and the CHURCH on the left; it may be signposted to Tala). You pass the village CEMETERY, on your left, after about 180m. At the end of Apis Street bear left at a roundabout and, at a T-junction (**15min**), turn left. You are now heading almost due north, walking past fruit and vegetable plots.

About 1km past the T-junction, turn left on a track signposted to the VILLAS KIKLAMINO and KLATSOPATIKA and lined on the left with TALL CONIFERS (**30min**). You will soon reach an area with a small WATER CONTROL POINT and a track junction with signs left to the two afore-mentioned villas. Here your track swings right alongside a WATER CHANNEL on the right (initially covered with concrete slabs). Follow this watercourse, with fine views over citrus groves as it heads inland.

At **50min** notice the cultivation below to your left and ignore a track to the right as you skirt orange groves. Pass a large gate just off to the right, as you head left along a fence on your right and zigzag down through orange trees. Some 150m short of an old shed, turn left through the citrus trees, away from the dam. When you join a rough metalled road, turn right uphill, climbing gently to the **Mavrokolymbos Dam** (Picnic 13; **1h25min**). Have a look at the steps, the sluice, a ruined building and an old bridge. A fine excuse for a breather!

Follow the track past the dam wall, and almost certainly see sheep and goats near the water's edge. About 500m/yds beyond the dam wall, at **1h30min**, turn sharp left on

74

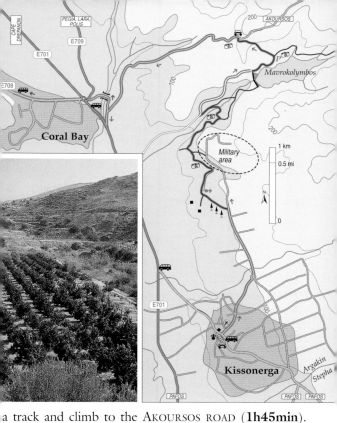

a track and climb to the AKOURSOS ROAD (**1h45min**).
Turn left: it's downhill almost all the way to the main road.
The nearest bus stop is to the *right*, on the far side of the
river, and buses are very frequent.

Or make for **Coral Bay** (**2h45min**) and take a dip!

*Above: citrus groves flourish in the valley below the Mavrokolymbos Dam. The
dam is a key part of the irrigation system for the agricultural industry around
Pafos. Below: Coral Bay*

Walk 14: LARA BEACH

See map and photographs on pages 78-79

Distance: 4km/2.5mi; 1h20min

Grade: easy

Equipment: stout shoes, sunhat, water, picnic, swimming things

How to get there and return: 🚗 car to/from Lara Beach, 27km north of Pafos via Coral Bay. The road is asphalted as far as a U-bend at the Aspros River; it then reverts to a wide unsurfaced road. Just 1.1km further on you'll see the signposted track to the Avagas Gorge on the right (Walk 16). After about 4km, beyond a sign to Lara Restaurant, the last 1km of track is very eroded — best done in a 4WD vehicle (or walked). Or 🚤 from Pafos (check at the tourist office for times)

Alternative walk: Avagas Gorge and Lara Beach (17km/10.5mi; 6h) Quite easy, but long. Park at the mouth of the Aspros River just north of Cape Drepanon (where the asphalt runs out). Walk into the Avagas Gorge (see Walk 16) and then on to Lara for this circuit. A great day out; worth putting the boots on!

Special note: Access may be restricted in July-August during the nesting season of the rare green turtle. Please observe relevant warning signs.

This attractive, unspoiled beach, setting for Picnic 14 can only be reached by car, or perhaps on a sea cruise out of Pafos during summer. By car it is a leisurely drive north, passing close to Coral Bay, then Agios Georgios. (A short detour here will show you an attractive fishing refuge and interesting church overlooking the sea.) The whole area dates back to Roman times and has been the scene of much excavation.

Thankfully, Lara has been spared the ravages of commerce; one can tolerate and even give thanks for the single seasonal restaurant near the beach which caters for most of Lara's visitors. Apart from the restaurant, there's absolutely nothing at Lara except wonderful coastal scenery and a quiet atmosphere. A most agreeable stroll can be made along and around the beach for an hour or two.

Start out near the LARA RESTAURANT at **Lara Beach**, walking down to the shoreline. At the north end of the beach is a headland crossed by tracks, offering very pleasing views south along the coast and inland to the hills north of Pegia. Close to Lara are the summer nesting grounds of the rare and protected green turtle.

North of Lara, the rough road gets even rougher before petering out after a few kilometres (see 4WD options for Car tour 1 on page 24), but there are some very secluded coves along here if you fancy skinny-dipping.

Thankfully, the Akamas Peninsula which includes the Lara region was made a national park area early in the 1990s, thus ensuring its continuing existence as a totally unspoiled, totally beautiful landscape.

Walk 15: FROM DROUSSEIA TO AGIOS GEORGIOS

See map pages 78-79; see photographs pages 17 and 80
Distance: 18km/11.2mi; about 5h
Grade: fairly easy but long, with a descent of about 600m/2000ft
Equipment: walking boots or stout shoes, sunhat, plenty of water, picnic, swimming things
How to get there: 🚌 to Polis (Timetable E5), then taxi to Drousseia (or with friends)
To return: 🚌 from Agios Georgios (Timetable E6)
Alternative walks: Masochists can link up Walk 14 or Short walk 16.

In the cooler months of spring and autumn it's most enjoyable to take a long Cyprus walk. This trek is quite easy, but choose a coolish day and carry plenty of water. There are no facilities of any kind on the route. The good news is that much of the walk is level or downhill (albeit on rough tracks), and the views over the whole Lara coastline will linger long in the memory.

Start out from **Drousseia**: follow *Alternative* walk 22 on page 96. When you reach the track (**30min**), turn right (past the modern church) and keep going until you come to the asphalted Androlikou–Kathikas road. Turn right here and, a short way along (just south of Pittokopos), turn left at a junction with a broad track (**50min**).

You now follow the roughest 'road' you're likely to find on Cyprus (4WD Option B in Car tour 1 bumps along here). After about 1km turn left, to start gaining views over the whole western coast around Lara Bay which is slightly to the left on the horizon. That is your target!

The way is simple, but don't rush it. Relish this *totally* unspoiled region, listen to the birdsong, smell the air, and take some wonderful photos as you follow the winding track gently downwards for some 7km, to join the rough road above **Lara**.

After visiting the beach (Walk 14), you have another 7km of walking on a similar road (past the turn-off to the **Avagas Gorge** and Walk 16). You should reach **Agios Georgios** in under **5h**, depending on your stride, and how many times you stop to take in the scenery. You'll be tired and thirsty, but you'll thank me for this wonderful experience of the Akamas... although perhaps not immediately!

Seen en route in the Akamas: perils of not wearing a sunhat?

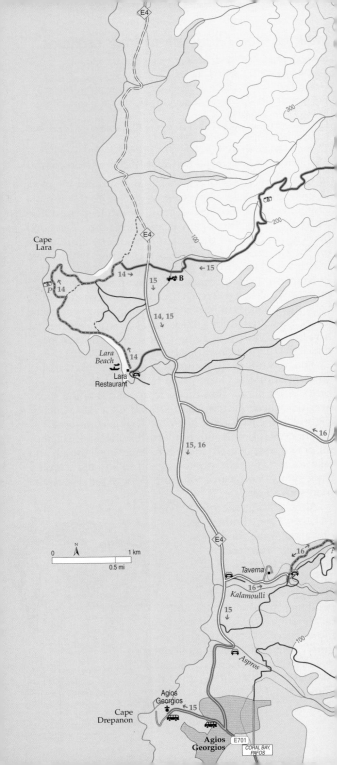

Walk 16: AVAGAS GORGE CIRCUIT

See map on pages 78-79   **Distance:** 17km/10.5mi, 5h15min

Grade: moderate-strenuous and long, with an ascent/descent of about 300m/1000ft. You must be sure-footed and agile: plenty of scrambling over slippery boulders as you criss-cross the stream bed; you must be sure-footed, and sometimes you'll need to use your hands. In winter the gorge may be *impassable,* if there is too much water. A good sense of direction is a help as you leave the gorge for the plateau above, and the long return on the motorable track is tiring, especially in hot weather.

Equipment: walking boots, sunhat, *plenty of* water, picnic, swimming things; in winter, a safety helmet is advisable (danger of rockfall!)

How to get there and return: 🚗 via Coral Bay and Agios Georgios, north of Pafos. Continue on track when the asphalt runs out 1.6km past Agios Georgios, and turn right 1.1km further on at a sign for the gorge (where there is a first car park). Keep ahead on the track, passing the drive up left to the Viklari Taverna after 550m, then turn left between two gateposts 400m further on, to a second car park with a noticeboard. Or 🚌 to/from Agios Georgios (Timetable E6), then 2.7km on foot

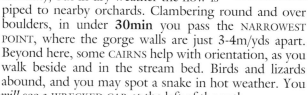

*Avagas Gorge: in the depths (right)
and on the plateau above (opposite)*

Short walk: Avagas Gorge (2km/1.2mi; 1h; fairly easy, but you must be sure-footed to sramble over the slippery boulders. Follow the main walk for about 30 minutes and return the same way. Perhaps explore the Kouphou Gorge — or the track between the two gorges — as well.

It's easy enough to venture into the Avagas Gorge from its mouth, walking only as far in as you feel comfortable (Short walk), but this circuit takes you up to the Laona Plateau for the beautiful views shown opposite.

Start out at the PARKING AREA. Walk through a gate to the left, into the northerly and most spectacular of the two ravines, the **Avagas Gorge**. Outside summer there should be ample water (in winter and early spring there may be too much...), but in dry weather the flow is piped to nearby orchards. Clambering round and over boulders, in under **30min** you pass the NARROWEST POINT, where the gorge walls are just 3-4m/yds apart. Beyond here, some CAIRNS help with orientation, as you walk beside in and in the stream bed. Birds and lizards abound, and you may spot a snake in hot weather. You *will* see a WRECKED CAR at the left of the path...

Ten minute past the wreck you pass a post painted with the number 48. Ignore a path on the right here; keep ahead, then soon take a narrow goats' path on the right (CAIRN), to climb up to the southern edge of the gorge. At the top, head left, more or less alongside the edge. Soon you'll see some old ruins ahead — a MILL and ANIMAL SHELTERS. Make for the mill: just after passing it, you pick up a track (**2h**) which bends left and takes you to the north side of the gorge. The track widens out, then joins the unsurfaced road between Lara and Kato Arodhes at a T-junction near more animal pens. Turn left.

You enjoy some splendid views from the high point of this motorable track. Ignore a lesser track off right, pass a small GOAT FARM on the right and, ignoring all turn-offs, just keep to the unsurfaced road as it descends through the Pegia Forest. At the T-junction with the unsurfaced coastal road (**4h**), turn left and walk along to the sign for the gorge. Then retrace the route you took by car, back to the PARKING AREA (**5h15min**).

81

Walk 17: KHAPOTAMI GORGE

Distance: 10km/6.2mi; 2h35min

Grade: moderate, with ascents of about 150m/500ft. It can be extremely hot in the gorge in high summer. *In early spring the walk may be impassable if there has been heavy rain and the river is running high.*

Equipment: walking boots or stout shoes, sunhat, plenty of water, picnic

How to get there: 🚌 (Timetable E10) or 🚕 taxi from Pafos to Pano Arkhimandrita

To return: 🚕 pre-arranged taxi from Alekhtora, or take the village taxi to the main road at Pissouri, from where you could telephone for a service taxi bound for Pafos or Lemesos.

Circular walk for motorists: Kato Arkhimandrita — Khapotami Gorge — Kato Arkhimandrita (7.5km/4.7mi; 2h30min; grade as main walk; note that the ascent at the end of the walk is in full sun and to be avoided in summer). 🚗 car to Pano Arkhimandrita. After viewing the shrine, drive back west to the village water tank and follow the sign 'Kato Arkhimandrita 2km', to drive down the rough road to the lower village. Pick up the main walk at the 45min-point and follow it to just past the 2h05min-point. Then take the *second* track off left, a wide vehicular track with a farm building 150m ahead on the left. It's a long, steady climb up here, with no shade, so take it easy. Part-way up you

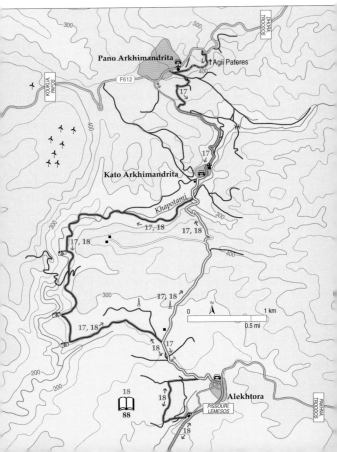

pass a pylon on the left. Close to the top of the ridge, the track sweeps 90 degrees to the left. Some 50m/yds further on, turn right to the brow (**2h**). Almost immediately after beginning the descent, take a stony path off left, which cuts off a bend in the track. Follow the track down to your car at Kato Arkhimandrita and (**2h30min**).

Pano Arkhimandrita is situated among vineyards perched on hillsides, and the effect of the scenery when you first arrive is quite breathtaking. There is more to come.

Clearly signed on the south side of the village is is a concrete road to 'The Cave of 318 Fathers'. Follow this and then go down some steps to the hermitage of Agii Pateres, a tiny shrine nestling in a rock crevice. Herein is preserved a quantity of human bones. It is said they are of 318 saints who arrived on the coast at Pissouri in days of yore after fleeing persecution in Syria, only to meet an untimely death at the hands of local heathens. Your welcome in Arkhimandrita will be warmer, especially in either of the two coffee shops where locals will happily talk about their tiny community.

Visit the SHRINE (see drawing above), respecting the 'don't touch' appeal, then **begin the walk** by scrambling down the slope alongside the telegraph pole to the earthen track just below. Follow this to the right as it hugs the side of the hill, ending just below the village church on a concrete road (**10min**). Turn left here and follow the concrete road downhill for three minutes, to a fork next to a small CHICKEN FARM. Head right here, downhill, until you come to another earthen track on your right (**15min**). Follow this track as it descends, then rises to a junction with an asphalt road (**20min**) — the old road to Kato Arkhimandrita.

Turn left now and head towards the village with the Arkhimandrita Valley on your left. When you reach the village of **Kato Arkhimandrita (45min)** you'll see that it's mostly abandoned to the goats, but a couple of the houses — and the church — have been restored. The inhabitants asked to leave and move to the upper village in the 1960s, because of their isolation (no good road, no school) and water supply problems. Walk through the

village, forking left in front of an inhabited house, and at
49min come to the river bed. It's usually dry, so you can
cross straight over, but there is a footbridge (for the
goats!) nearby. On the far side of the river bed take the
track to the right.

Beyond an open area (**1h10min**) you are heading into
the spectacular **Khapotami Gorge**. Towering cliffs, birds
of prey wheeling overhead, an infinite variety of trees and

plants, lizards scampering at your feet … the holiday beaches seem a long way from this kind of Cyprus. Follow the track — sometimes just the boulders of the river bed *(and totally impassable when the river is running high in winter or spring)* — as it runs all the way through the walkable part of the gorge. At about **1h35min**, at a fork, your track widens and heads up to the left, out of the gorge. (The track to the right crosses the river and zigzags

up the opposite side of the gorge; ignore the track heading sharply back to the left.) You will get ever more impressive views down into the impassable part of the gorge as you climb.

Eventually, the track levels out and contours round two sharp left-hand bends, the gorge always on your right. Notice a pylon up to the left in the distance and rise gently to pass through two gates, into a vineyard (**2h05min**). *(For the Circular walk,* ignore *the first track off left, 60m past the second gate; take the* next, wide *track to the left, 130m further on.)* The main walk continues ahead for somewhat over 1km into **Alekhtora** (**2h35min**).

Top: priest at Pano Arkhi-mandrita (left) and wall painting inside his church (middle); church in the ruined village of Kato Arkhimandrita (right). Left: Arkhimandrita's green valley

Walk 18: CIRCUIT FROM ALEKHTORA

Distance: 10km/6.2mi; 3h05min (or shorten by almost 5km/1h35min by driving — in an ordinary car — to the antenna at the 50min-point)

Grade: quite easy, with a climb/descent of about 125m/400ft

Equipment: walking boots or stout shoes, sunhat, water, picnic

How to get there and return: 🚌 take the F611 north from Pissouri to the junction near the sign 'Alekhtora 1km', where the road makes a near-90° right turn, next to a fruit-packing factory (see map on page 88).

Alternative walk: Alekhtora — Lakko tou Frankou — Khapotami Gorge — Alekhtora (17km/10.6mi; 5h30min; strenuous and long, with ascents/descents of about 400m/1300ft). Equipment and access as main walk; *take plenty of water. Not suitable in high summer,* as there is almost no shade. Combine this walk with Walk 17 for a long day out. After this walk, head north along the road towards Alekhtora for 1km. Just past a disused fruit-packing shed on the left, fork left on a track running behind the back of the shed, ignoring the narrow road to the right. Ignore a track off left and another right; take the *next* track to the right, 500m from the shed. Skirting vineyards on the right, head north for 600m. Then turn right for 400m, to meet the vehicle track followed at the end of Walk 17. Turn left and after 0.8km/half a mile, follow this track uphill to the right, ignoring another wide track to the left (you will see a farm building 150m/yds ahead to the left and a pylon on the left further uphill). Close to the top of the ridge, the track sweeps 90° left. Some 50m/yds further on, turn right to the brow. Almost immediately into the descent, take a stony path off left, which cuts off a bend in the track. Follow the track down to the abandoned village of Kato Arkhimandrita. Now pick up Walk 17 at the 45min-point, to walk through the Kapotami Gorge and back towards Alekhtora, picking up your outward track round the vineyards and turning right at the disused fruit-packing shed, back to your car.

This is an interesting walk, mainly through farming land. The old hamlet of Lakko tou Frankou provides a fascinating insight into life past and, if you haven't already done Walk 17, the spectacular views into the gorge will surely whet your appetite for it.

Start out at the junction by the 'ALEKHTORA' sign. Follow a surfaced track through vineyards and a few olive groves. Go straight on at a junction (**12min**), still gently climbing. You pass another fruit-packing depot and an ENCLOSURE sheltering goats with with longest,

Goat enclosure typical of the island's interior

floppiest ears your're ever likely to see! The track soon starts zigzagging up to the antenna visible above. Make use of short-cuts and reach the top at the solar-powered ANTENNA (**45min**, Picnic 18a). Have a breather, if not a picnic, and survey the countryside you have just traversed.

Follow the track northwest uphill towards some sheds. As you can see on the map, we're heading for an overview of the Khapotami Gorge, the setting for Walk 17. Goats graze amongst the carob trees, and large flocks of jack-daws screech noisily. After a few minutes you approach the large ENCLOSURE OF GOAT SHEDS (**1h**) where you should bear left. Take the track running westwards, walking through carob trees and keeping the large wind turbines above the gorge to your right. After five minutes, bear left at a minor junction and you will see, above the trees on the hillside ahead, a large animal farm in the distance. You are headed for this; always keep the wind turbines on your right. When you reach the ANIMAL FARM (**1h20min**), take the track which heads down along its left-hand side. Step down through old stone terraces to the KHAPOTAMI OVERLOOK (**1h32min**; Picnic 18b), for really spectacular views into the Khapotami Gorge.

When you have enjoyed a break in these beautiful surroundings, walk back about 30m/yds past the animal farm and, facing away from both it and the ridge, take an

indistinct grassy track heading southeast into sparse pine woods. Head for a triangulation point — a white stone cairn about a metre high and painted with a large black '9'. From this reference point walk just a few metres southeast to a wide track and follow this to the right (south) downhill. The rough track descends and takes you to a tiny church, **Agios Georgios** (**1h52min**). It has white walls, a faded red roof and no windows.

Immediately beyond the church is an 18th-century 'KHAN' or coaching station. Just beyond this the track comes to a junction, where a stone trough sits beside an OLD WELL (now dry). This perhaps gave rise to this area's name of **Lakkou tou Frankou** (Well of the French). Turn sharp left at this junction and in two minutes pass a RIDING CLUB on your right. The vehicle track rises gradually (it used to be cobbled in places, indicating that this was perhaps an important trans-village link in bygone days). When you reach the antenna junction of your outward route (**2h25min**), don't forget the short-cuts for your descent. Say 'hello' to the long-eared goats and return to your car at the 'ALEKHTORA' sign (**3h05min**).

Walk 19: FONTANA AMOROSA COASTAL PATH

See map on reverse of touring map; see also photographs on pages 90 and 92

Distance: 6km/3.7mi, 1h45min

Grade: quite easy, almost level walking

Equipment: stout shoes, sunhat, water, picnic, swimming things

How to get there and return: 🚗 car or 🚐 (Timetable F1) to/from Lakki, then ⛵ from Lakki to Fontana Amorosa; 🚐 (Timetable F1) or taxi from the Baths of Aphrodite back to Lakki

A wonderful walk with amazing views around the compass. Birdsong, butterflies, tiny lizards avoiding your feet, and a backdrop of mountains. What more could one ask for? This walk takes you through unspoiled Cyprus, and long may it remain so.

The best approach to Fontana Amorosa is from the sea, so head initially to Lakki, where a boat can be hired to take you there (ask at the Lakki Water Sports Centre). Sharing the boat journey with others will ensure that the cost is very reasonable. There is no proper landing area; the boatman will ask you to leap ashore on a hot and rocky outcrop which, at first sight, hardly merits its name. In reality the 'fountain of love' is a 5-metre deep well (which you may not even find), but it doesn't matter! You have only come for the pleasure of walking back to the Baths of Aphrodite. For a longer ramble, it is interesting to walk to the very western tip of the island, Cape Arnauti (an extra 3km/2mi return; always keeping to paths nearest the sea), passing the wrecked freighter Agnello on the way.

The track from **Fontana Amorosa starts out** in an area of scrub. It may take a minute to locate, but once found, there is no problem. Simply head back eastwards and enjoy the environment. The route wanders through scrub on both sides, but in **10min** you should be enjoying good views of the sea. In **20min** come to a large WARNING SIGN ABOUT MILITARY EXERCISES and take good notice: don't touch anything suspicious-looking. Equally, don't be deterred by the 'red flag' aspect of this walk. It really is spectacular, with no evidence of the military, except for the signs.

At **40min** the track turns inland for no more than 50m/yds to avoid a gully, then it gains height as it continues eastwards. At about **45min** you may catch sight of a cairn on a rock to the right, and of a particularly attractive cove down left. At **1h10min** the route climbs more steeply, but not for long, and the views from this level are the finest of the walk. At the end

89

of this stretch, one gets a panoramic view over the **Baths of Aphrodite**, which should be reached in about **1h45min**. For this last descent, keep to the broader track on the right, not the narrower way through low-lying trees… lest you disturb the goats.

From the Baths you can catch a bus back to Lakki in summer, or call for a taxi when you arrive. You *could* even walk to Lakki along shingle beaches and the edges of fields, but the way is unclear, the going frustrating, and the landscape indifferent compared with what has gone before.

Left: wild garlic flourishes in stony areas.
Below: a delightfully secluded cove, seen from above the Baths of Aphrodite; the camping site is nicely situated on the cliffs in the background.

Walk 20: THE 'APHRODONIS' TRAIL

See map on reverse of touring map; see also photographs opposite and on pages 17 and 95 (bottom)

Distance: about 7.5km/4.7mi; 2h50min, whichever trail you choose

Grade: moderate, with a steep climb of 250m/820ft at the start. The Aphrodite trail climbs an additional 100m/330ft. Both trails involve zigzag descents on fairly loose rubble in places; *you must be sure-footed and have a head for heights.*

Equipment: stout shoes or boots, sunhat, water, picnic; optional trekking pole(s)

How to get there and return: 🚗 car or taxi to/from the Baths of Aphrodite restaurant car park. Or 🚌 from Polis (Timetable F1)

Walkers who have trod the Fontana Amorosa coastal path (Walk 19) know how special the views are in this 'top left-hand corner' of Cyprus. Imagine how much more exciting those views are from 300 metres (1000 feet) higher up! Thanks to a pair of Forestry Department nature trails ('Aphrodite' and 'Adonis'), you can enjoy these views and at the same time learn more about the flora and fauna of the Akamas. A booklet explaining points of interest, and a large-scale map, are usually available from the Polis tourist office.

The two trails share a common ascent at the start, lasting a little over an hour. The Aphrodite trail then heads northwest, climbing to skirt the Moutti tis Sotiras plateau, and offers incomparable views towards Cape Arnauti. The Adonis trail heads in the opposite direction initially, giving splendid views over the coastline southeast of the Baths of Aphrodite. I take you up to the 'decision point', then describe both trails. Whichever you choose, you're likely to come back and head the opposite way another day!

You need more than sandals or trainers for either experience, for while the routes are well marked and by no means severe, they do present some challenge to wind and limb, and the surfaces can be rocky or loose, especially on their zigzag descents (some 'Landscapers' have experienced mild vertigo on the Aphrodite descent).

The walk starts at the CAR PARK close to the CTO RESTAURANT. Head west to the clearly signed start to the trails. You reach **Loutra Aphroditis** (the **Baths of Aphrodite**) at TRAIL POINT 5; Aphrodite was said to sport with lovers here. Follow the sign 'NATURE TRAIL', crossing the bed of the **Argaki tou Pyrgou** and heading up steps. The coastal track from Fontana Amorosa (Walk 19), your return route, is below. Go through a turnstile and look up left to see two WHITE CONCRETE CAIRNS; head sharp left up to the highest cairn (painted with the number '2'. Keeping this to your right, follow the steep path to a third cairn — at TRAIL POINT 8 (**15min**). Keep left at another fork two minutes later.

As you rise, you'll notice a small island with a cross, which commemorates a diver who lost his life near the island some years ago. About 50m past TRAIL POINT 10 you are directed sharply up to the right, and you very soon come to TRAIL POINT 11. There are seats near here from where you can enjoy your first really good views over the coast (**35min**; Picnic 20, photograph page 17). Walk through a clearing which is level for about 200m/yds, but

Cape Arnauti from the Aphrodite trail

ahead you'll see (and feel!) the trail rising sharply. It can be a sweat, but the pain doesn't last long! At the top there's a welcome bench, from which to look back to Lakki and beyond to Polis.

At a fork beyond TRAIL POINT 20 turn left. You will come to a large wooded hollow with a GIANT OAK TREE and the substantial remains of **Pyrgos tis Rigaenas** (Queen's Shelter; **1h10min**, photograph page 95), believed to be the site of a medieval monastery. Nearby is a welcome SPRING (but it *may* be dry in summer). This is another excellent area for picnicking (Picnic 20), while you decide which of the trails to follow — **Aphrodite or Adonis**; both are signposted from the hollow (as is another nature trail, Smigies, which is followed in Walk 21).

Aphrodite (A25 to A49): Follow the signposted track which rises in a northerwesterly direction. After TRAIL POINT A30 leave the track on a short-cut path to the right, passing a flourish of rock roses. Following signs, zigzag up to TRAIL POINT A35. (If you continue a few yards up the track here, a path from the vehicle turning area leads to a viewpoint on the **Moutti tis Sotiras** plateau.) But you will have equally stunning view towards Cape Arnauti from TRAIL POINT A37, as you zigzag down the narrowing path. *Take care* where the surface is loose. You join the coastal track from Fontana Amorosa at around **2h20min** and pass another SPRING a few minutes later. After a short climb you finish up back at the RESTAURANT at the **Baths of Aphrodite** (**2h50min**). This is a marvellous walk at any time of year, but in spring you may have the bonus of spotting the Cyprus tulip.

Adonis (B25 to B55): The trail climbs a short distance, past juniper trees. Near POINT B29 you briefly join a forestry road; keep left downhill. Beyond a fine stand of Calabrian pines (TRAIL POINT B30), keep left downhill on a path, leaving the track. When you come to TRAIL POINT B34 (**1h45min**), turn left (the way straight ahead also leads to the Smigies trail and Walk 21). There's a WATER TROUGH here, of alleged drinking quality, but you may prefer your bottle. There's a really lovely descent now, to the right of a gully, and the whole area is covered with wild flowers in spring. Simply follow the trail numbers (there's a long gap between B46 and B47). At TRAIL POINT B50 you come to a stunning viewpoint with a bench, from where you can see your zigzag descent. At the bottom, turn left on the road, back to the **Baths of Aphrodite** (**2h50min**).

Walk 21: AKAMAS GOLD

Map on reverse of touring map   **Distance**: 13km/8mi; 3h30min

Grade: moderate, with ascents of about 250m/820ft

Equipment: walking boots or stout shoes, sunhat, water, picnic, *torch*

How to get there and return: 🚗 car or taxi to/from Neo Chorio (via Lakki); there are also buses from Polis, but timings are not convenient.

Short walk for motorists: Smigies nature trail (6.5km/4mi; 2h; easy). Drive on the rough road out of Neo Chorio to the Smigies picnic site (see map; signposted) and start and end the walk there.

Even shorter walk for motorists: Do the Short walk above, but turn off the ridge track at nature trail signpost No 9, where there is a sign 'Smigies 2km'.

Alternative walks: Below are just two possibilities from the many walk options in this area (see map on reverse of touring map). Take a taxi to start; return from the Baths by 🚐 (Timetable F1).

1   **Neo Chorio — Smigies — Aphrodite trail — Baths of Aphrodite** (13km/8mi; 3h15min; an additional climb of 100m/330ft). After visiting the mine (1h30min), retrace your steps to the ridge track and continue along it, then turn right at a military warning sign to link up with the Aphrodite trail (Walk 20). When you reach it, near trail point A35, pick up the notes on page 93 to climb round the Moutti tis Sotiras plateau and then descend to the Baths. (You could also turn *right* on the trail and descend more directly to the Baths from Pyrgos tis Rigaenas.)

2   **Neo Chorio — Smigies — Adonis trail — Baths of Aphrodite** (10km/6.2mi; 2h30min). From the mine, continue on the Smigies nature trail, then join the Adonis nature trail near point No B34. Keep ahead to descend to the Baths.

Is it a gold mine? Or was it just magnesium ore that Cypriot miners extracted from the abandoned workings we find on this grand route? Let's go see, but don't give up the day job yet! The real rewards on this day's outing are the magnificent views over Chrysochou (Golden) Bay and the Akamas Forest in the south.

Start out at the CHURCH in **Neo Chorio**. Walk west along the road to some WATER TANKS on the edge of the village, just beyond which the road forks (**10min**). Head right here, towards Agios Minas. The left fork would take you to the goats of Androlikou (see page 24)… another day, perhaps? Beyond the restored church of **Agios Minas** (**40min**) the concrete road reverts to track and you come to the popular **Smigies** PICNIC SITE (**50min**; Picnic 21). Keep to the left of it*, passing the start of a signposted circuit round the **Pissouromouti** peak. (This optional detour, including a climb to the top, would give you a magnificent view over the whole coast: allow 3km/2mi and an extra 125m/400ft of ascent; 1h.)

*My route picks up the Smigies nature trail at point 9; if you prefer to follow the route from the start, walk down into the picnic site to join the path (shown in yellow on the map) at the left of the trail sign.

Some say this abandoned mine once produced gold... but old maps indicate magnesium. Whatever the end product, this is the old smelter, opposite the galleried workings of the mine.
Below: Pyrgos tis Rigaenas
(Alternative walk and Walk 20)

Come at **55min** to a T-junction of tracks on a ridge ('Route A' in the 4WD Options for Car tour 1 on page 24). Turn right and start enjoying the views, firstly to the left, and later, in both directions. There'll likely be a welcome breeze, even on a hot day. You pass the turn-off to a FIRE-WATCH STATION, then come to a signpost back to 'Smigies 2km — Short Way' on your right *(the 'Even shorter walk')*. Having joined the **Smigies nature trail**, keep ahead for 500m/yds, to a level track on the right rounding the hillside. *Ignore* this but, 150m further on, turn right on a track marked with a GREEN ARROW. It drops sharply to the right, passes a large ruined shelter on the left and leads to the ABANDONED MINES (**1h 30min**). On the left is the smelting furnace (what's left of

it), ahead is a short-cut to your ongoing path and, to the right, entrances to the old galleries. *If you have a torch*, you might explore for a short way, but take care (there are deep pits inside!), and don't venture in alone.

You now have several options.

For the main walk, walk back a few paces and follow the track that descends to the left of the smelter (GREEN ARROW) then, at TRAIL POINT 14 (turpentine tree), turn hard right (almost back the way you came) and follow the path gently uphill. Soon you join a track and can see the church of Agios Minas ahead to the left. The track leads back to the PICNIC SITE (**2h40min**), from where you can retrace your steps to **Neo Chorio** (**3h30min**).

For Alternative walk 1, return to the ridge track as described above, to reach the **Aphrodite trail** northwest of Pyrgos tis Rigaenas, then see notes on page 93.

For Alternative walk 2 continue as the main walk, but keep *left* past trail point 14, to reach the **Adonis trail** near a SPRING and SIGNPOST B34; then see notes on page 93.

A great day's walking, whatever your choice of routes.

Walk 22: KRITOU TERRA AND TERRA

Distance: 4km/2.5mi, 1h30min

Grade: easy descent/reascent of about 150m/500ft, but the path down to the stream is *very difficult in spring, demanding careful footwork*.

Equipment: stout shoes, sunhat, water, picnic

How to get there and return: 🚌 to/from Kritou Terra (a detour on Car tour 1, page 23). Park near the village springs/disused taverna at the entrance to the village. (There are buses from both Pafos and Polis, but current timings are inconvenient.)

Alternative walk: Drousseia circuit (3.5km/2.2mi; 1h; easy, with an ascent/descent of just 40m/130ft). An ideal leg-stretcher, all on concrete and tarmac and suitable for sandals. 🚌 to Drousseia (there are buses from both Pafos and Polis, but timings are inconvenient); park behind the Droushia Heights Hotel. Walk up into the village, passing Finikas Tavera. Turn right between two coffee houses (signed 'Palates Apartments'), descending to the open-air theatre. Go straight ahead on Odos Karis (signed in Greek) and turn left on concrete at a yellow E4 arrow (15min). You get fantastic views of the Troodos Mountains and the north coast and pass an interesting rock outcrop (25min; Picnic 22). Carry on via vineyards, to a T-junction (30min). Your way is to the left, but first walk a short way to the right (the route of Walk 15) — to a tiny modern church. Then return and, now on tarmac, regain Drousseia (1h).

This is a lovely, short and very interesting stroll. Kritou Terra's fortunes are improving: once home to 800 souls, its population fell to just 100. But the opening of an Environmental Studies Centre in the old primary school was a turning point, with some 2000 international students visiting each year.

Start out at the entrance to **Kritou Terra**: take the middle road, between the SPRINGS (left) and an old MILL-STONE (right). Midway through the village, as the road bends round and up to the right, you reach a large BLUE SIGNBOARD indicating the way to a number of points of interest. Leave the main road here and fork straight ahead towards St Chryseleousa church, St George's church and the waterfall, amongst others. (The right turn leads to the church shown opposite.) On the left here is the vine-covered former FLOUR MILL. If you look over the low wall beyond it, you will see a series of holes in the rock beside a water channel — the old COMMUNAL LAUNDRY.

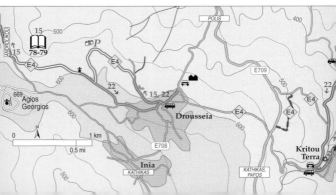

Top: the Byzantine church of Agia Ekaterina lies not far from Drousseia and the Terras. Since this medieval ruin is more complete than many on Cyprus and contains some faded wall paintings, it is well worth a short (5km) detour during Car tour 1. To reach it, take the crudely signposted road from Kritou Terra (see map — not the Terra road). The church can also be reached within 2km from the Pafos–Polis road at a marked turn-off 1km south of Skoulli.
Left: these beautiful springs in Terra were a communal gathering place.

At the end of the village, pass the CHURCH (and road to the Environmental Studies Centre) on the right, then ignore two concrete roads off right (the second rises to a small chapel). You can see Terra ahead. Some 100m past the chapel, *before* the driveway to a house on the left, watch for a long METAL GRATING across the road. Just beyond this, and directly in front of a telegraph pole, turn hard left on a very overgrown path — almost invisible in spring and *slippery after rain*. Bear with this path for a couple of minutes, then zigzag steeply down to the valley floor.

After crossing a streambed, the path widens out. Ignore any lesser turn-offs and keep the nearby streambed on your right. As the path turns to concrete and veers right, you pass a large CONCRETE WATER TANK on your left. Go left at the next T-junction. Bend round to the right past the springs shown above and (now on asphalt) come to the old MOSQUE in **Terra** (**45min**) — without minaret, but with cypress trees 'guarding' it. There has been a settlement here since Roman times. Nowadays some of the Turkish-owned houses abandoned during the 1974 occupation of the north are being restored by Greeks. Keep to the left of the mosque, to walk to the north of the village. Reaching a T-junction after about 300m, turn left and follow the road back to **Kritou Terra** (**1h30min**).

Distance: 10.5km/6.5mi; 2h55min

Grade: strenuous, with steep ascents/descents (300m/1000ft overall). All tracks are good, if muddy after rain. The *multiplicity* of tracks can lead to doubts, but the map is precise (GPS tracks are available to download).

Equipment: walking boots or stout shoes, sunhat, picnic, water; trekking poles useful

How to get there and return: 🚗 to/from Miliou, a detour from the 83km-point on Car tour 1. Shortly before Miliou, pass the Agii Anargyri Hotel, then park in a small lay-by just after crossing a bridge with iron railings. (There is also a bus from Polis, but timings are inconvenient.)

Short walk: Miliou views (2.5km/1.6mi; 45min; easy, with an ascent/ descent of only 60m/200ft). Follow the main walk to the 25min-point, enjoy the splendid views, and return the same way.

This is a glorious hike with far-reaching views, sometimes over the whole walk route. The deserted village of Kato Theletra is fascinating to explore and provides a welcome shady pause before the second leg of the walk. *Be sure to follow the instructions carefully* — the whole area is cultivated and covered with a myriad of tracks.

Start the walk at the LAY-BY in **Miliou**: head back the way you came, climb up past the AGII ANARGYRI HOTEL, and notice the high ridge overlooking the valley to the right. The return route runs along the ridge, a little below the top. Look out also for resident peregrine falcons, easily identified by their alternate flapping and gliding.

As the road bends sharp left go straight ahead on a concrete track (**8min**). At a Y-fork 200m from the road, old Kato Theletra is visible in the distance, with the church of new Pano Theletra perched above it — and the whole walk is laid out before you. Go right here and descend the concrete track into the **Neradhes Valley**. Cross the watercourse ('Stream of the Fairies'; **14min**), then bear right and start climbing, ignoring tracks off left and right. Some 350m/yds up from the watercourse (**21min**), on an uphill bend to the right, take the lesser track off left — *that is, keeping straight on*. Continue up to a minor junction of tracks (**25min**). To the left are panoramic views across groves to the hills, with the village of Yiolou just visible on the ridge (Picnic 23). *(The Short walk turns back here.)*

Continue straight ahead on the main route and within about 250m/yds, at a fork (where the track you are on curves left, back towards the Neradhes Valley), go uphill to the right (**29min**), passing a Wildlife Conservation Area sign on the left. Ignore a clear track off left after 70m. At a Y-fork after a further 200m (on crossing a small gully), stay left, and soon start to descend towards the Neradhes Gorge. Stay left at the next Y-fork (**36min**), and

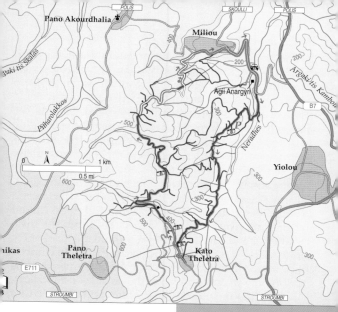

do the same again after another 200m, heading down between almond groves and vineyards. Cross a narrow ravine (**44min**) and, at the next fork, go left downhill. A LARGE HOUSE across the valley on your left confirms your route. Follow the main track as it crosses the fertile **Neradhes** streambed, lined with giant reeds (**48min**). Go straight on at a junction, following the streambed. This damp area, where there is sometimes a sizeable pool, attracts birds. At a fork, go uphill to the left and undulate gently alongside the stream, eventually crossing it again. The track (sometimes concreted) then zigzags steeply uphill. *Be sure to take the sharp left uphill track at a hairpin bend* (**56min**). Pause often to admire the surroundings and catch your breath.

Gourds; Kato Theletra

99

The track levels out a bit and you reach the road through **Kato Theletra** (**1h09min**). The ongoing walk turns up sharp right here, but you will surely wish to explore. Most houses are still deserted, but some are being restored and there are often locals around, tending the vines and other fruit trees. As you continue the walk uphill on a wide asphalt road, marvel at the extent of the Troodos Mountains across the valley. Where the road bends sharp left (**1h18min**), leave it on a concrete downhill track straight ahead (by electricity pole number L3-36-21-8). The track soon reverts to dirt and follows the gorge, passing a deserted smallholding. Ignore all tracks off left and right to groves and the like. At **1h25min** the main track makes a U-turn to the right around the head of the gorge; follow it as it heads briefly eastwards and climbs a concrete section. Go right at a Y-fork, opposite the smallholding passed earlier (on the far side of the valley).

Follow the main track, sometimes concreted, past a track going down right to a rocky outcrop. As you now contour around the slopes you'll see the village of Yiolou over to the right, backed by Mount Olympus. On reaching a SMALL OPEN AREA (**1h39min**) ignore the track going back sharp right, and after just a few metres fork left uphill. Ignore minor tracks and follow the main track to another fork after 100m. Bear right here. Contour round fertile terracing, past vineyards on the left.

As the track you left earlier comes in from the left, continue down a rather rough, stony track (**1h49min**). Cross a dip and rise steeply to a multiple junction (**2h05min**). Ignore the track off 90° left; take the concreted downhill track straight ahead, with a telegraph pole on your left. Notice Miliou below to the right. Continue downhill on a sometimes concreted, sometimes stony track. As it bends slightly right, notice a STONE HUT on your left, just before a small crossroads. Continue straight ahead here, following the track down towards a couple of small concrete ELECTRICITY PLANTS next to a telegraph pole. The track winds to the right here, descending gradually round the gorge. A group of concrete WATER TANKS on your left (**2h20min**) confirms your route.

Ten minutes later you arrive at the asphalt road from Pano Akourdhalia, coming in from the left. Walk down this road and reach the first houses in **Miliou** (**2h 36min**). You pass the friendly village coffee house/restaurant off to your left. Continue straight on, winding downhill and out of the village, back to the LAY-BY (**2h55min**).

Walk 24: ALAMANOU TO GOVERNOR'S BEACH

Distance: 5-8km/3-5mi; 1h30min-2h10min

Grade: very easy, but sometimes rough underfoot; *no shade: best walked from November to April*

Equipment: stout shoes, sunhat, water, swimwear

How to get there: 🚗 car to Agios Georgios Alamanou or to a large parking area by the shore, south of the monastery. Or 🚌 (Timetables B6, C5) to the Agios Georgios Alamanou turn-off on the old road between Lemesos and Larnaka.

To return: 🚌 from the old main road above Governor's Beach (Timetables B6, C5) — back to the Agios Georgios Alamanou turn-off, from where you can walk to your car, or back to base. Or taxi back to your car. There is also a 🚌 which runs from Governor's Beach to the waterfront hotels in Lemesos between May and September: check up-to-date times with a tourist office.

Note: If travelling by bus, reconfirm with a tourist office or the operator that the buses you plan to use are travelling on the old road and will stop at the monastery turn-off and the beach.

If Governor's Beach were white or golden in colour, developers would have had their way with it by now. But its grey (though clean) appearance has saved this popular retreat from touristic blandness. No one would include it in a list of the world's great watering-holes, but its informal — even ramshackle — atmosphere makes for a happy finish to this easiest of strolls. The walk can be accomplished with ease in either direction, but hire-car drivers might find it most agreeable to start at the

The blue and white galleries and courtyard at the monastery of Agios Georgios Alamanou: the sisters here sell flowers, jam, eggs and chickens, and a lone monk occupies a single room near the entrance, wherein he eats, sleeps, and paints icons which the visitor can buy.

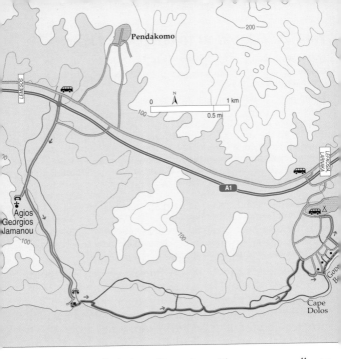

monastery of Agios Georgios Alamanou, walk to Governor's Beach for a swim and lunch, then return. The monastery is not particularly ancient, but its blue and white galleries and courtyard are very pretty, as you can see in the photograph on page 101.

To **start the walk** at **Agios Georgios Alamanou**, take the road off to the right just back from the monastery car park. (Since this road can be heavily trafficked in summer, you may prefer to drive down to the car park by the coast to begin.) On foot, you reach the sea and a shingle beach in about **30min**; there is a good fish taverna here (closed from early December to the end of February). Turn left along the beach for a few minutes, then climb briefly onto a track which frays its way along to Governor's Beach, generally hugging the waterline.

I like to approach the **Governor's Beach** area by first rising a bit up the headland at **Cape Dolos**, to survey the scene and then descend to the signposted tavernas — of which there are several. Your journey from the monastery should take about **1h45min**.

From here walk on about 1km to the junction with the old coastal road, where you can flag down a bus in either direction. Or call for a taxi to take you back to your car, if the effort of lunch has been too much!

Walk 25: KELLAKI TO PHINIKARIA

Distance: 12.5km/7.8mi; 3h15min

Grade: moderate; you should be sure-footed and have a head for heights. Ascent 240m/790ft; descent 500m/1640ft

Equipment: stout shoes or boots, sunhat, water, picnic

How to get there: 🚌 to Kellaki (Timetable B11); alight 1.6km south of the village, at the junction with the road to Prastio.
To return: 🚌 from Phinikaria to Lemesos (Timetable B10)

Short walk: Phinikaria fisherman's trail (1.5km/0.9mi; 30min or more; easy — trainers will suffice). Drive across the wall of Germasogia Dam and on to the signposted nature trail: as you enter Phinikaria turn left on a small road which skirts the very edge of the reservoir until you come to a small car park on your left where the road bends uphill to the right. Walk down from the car park to an information board and map (missing at press date!). It will take about 30 minutes to walk the circuit around the peninsula (a little over 1km), but it is also worth climbing the steps to the hexagonal shelter on the central hill (Picnic 25a).

Alternative circuits for motorists

1 Circuit below Kyparissia (8.5km/5.3mi; 2h40min; moderate, with an ascent/descent of 200m/650ft; you should be sure-footed and have a head for heights). 🚗 Drive to the junction at the start of the main walk and drive along road, then forest road, following instructions for the main walk for about 2km, to the 31min-point. Park here, neatly, and continue following the main walk to the 1h41min-point (1h10min). Turn sharp right uphill and climb through thinning pines. Wind round the slopes, rising gradually with ever-changing views. Pass a bench just after a sharp right turn and almost immediately come to a junction. Turn sharp right here; a rocky track takes you steeply up to a fork. Go right and reach a secondary peak of Kyparissia, where there is a hexagonal wooden shelter (1h38min, Picnic 25b). Views in all directions give you a matchless panorama — from Mount Olympus in the north to the dam in the south, Kouklia in the west and the mountains above Larnaka in the east. Continue downhill on this track, walking under the main peak of Kyparissia. You will reach a bench where the track forks. Take the left fork, to complete the loop at the 4-way junction (1h55min). Then take the wide track of your outward route, to return to your car (2h40min).

Kellaki

2   Circuit from Germasogia Dam (13.5km/8.4mi; 4h; quite strenu-ous, with an ascent/descent of 590m/1935ft). You should be sure-footed and have a head for heights. Although most of this walk is out and back, it is a brilliant hike, much of it on mountain paths — a proper hiker's day out. Drive to the car park for the Short walk. Walk up the asphalt road opposite (Lapithou Street) and after 12 minutes turn off left on Kyparissouvouno Street (there may be a green hikers sign). This is the 2h48min-point of the main walk; referring to the map, follow the main walk in reverse back to its 1h41min-point (the path off left below Kyparissia, marked by a hikers sign) and then pick up the notes for *Alternative* walk 1. When you reach the 4-way junction, pick up the main walk again at the 1h18min-point and follow it back to your car (4h).

O n this walk you'll pass from rugged mountainside to gentle countryside enjoying the varied scenery — a deep gorge, a vast (but perhaps dry) dam and splendid views. On the heights there are plenty of kestrels and partridges; lower down, the mixed vegetation, water and nearby houses make a fine habitat for small birds like coal tits, goldfinches, blackcaps and Sardinian warblers.

Start the walk on the E109 road at the junction sign-posted to Prastio, 1.6km south of Kellaki. Follow the road

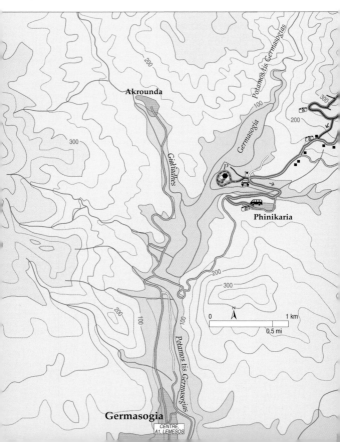

downhill for 350m/yds, ignoring the right turn to Prastio. Continue on road for another 400m/yds, then turn left (due south) on a forestry road where there is a signpost 'KYPARISSIA NATURE TRAIL 2.5KM'. Ignore all turn-offs and keep on this motorable track, eventually passing a little house on the left and coming to a major junction of forestry tracks (just under 2km; **31min**). Fork right, uphill, here. *(Alternative walk 1 drives to this point and joins the main walk.)* You are now climbing on a steep rough track with sheer drops down left into the valley. Pause to take in the magnificent views.

Reach a junction with signs and a bench, the official start of the **Kyparissia trail (56min)**. Follow the trail and the GREEN HIKERS SIGN left past the information board and walk sharp left uphill. You'll almost feel you are climbing to the stars! But the way soon levels out (**1h11min**) and brings you to a 4-WAY JUNCTION, also with a bench

(**1h18min**). Follow the arrow pointing downhill, almost straight ahead. You pass a track joining from the right as your track becomes a path and descends more steadily. Notice the first of the very few tree identification signs on the left and then look up to the right to see the hexagonal shelter visited on Alternative walk 1 (**1h29min**; Picnic 25b). After a few short zigzags walk alongside a stream bed, then cross it (**1h36min**). Continue alongside the stream and after a short rise notice a narrow path going back up to the right, indicated by a GREEN HIKERS SIGN (**1h41min**). *(Alternative walk 1 takes this path.)*

Continue ahead. The path begins to descend more sharply and becomes more rocky. You'll soon catch your first views of the **Kyparissia Gorge** (the northerly arm of the Germasogia River) to the right. Wind down through pines and pause to look down to the dam and all the way past Lemesos to the Akrotiri Peninsula (**1h52min**). The path continues to descend and switches to the left side of the ridge for a while, but then back to the right as it descends to meet a track where two HIKERS SIGNS point back the way you have come (**2h11min**). Turn left, downhill.

Get closer views of the dam and reservoir and in a few minutes pass a track coming in from the left. You will then find yourself heading east, away from the dam, as you begin a long zigzag. But don't worry, you'll soon change direction again as you follow this wide track. At **2h25min**

a track signposted 'Phinikaria 3km' heads down to the right — an optional short-cut which rejoins the walk at the 2h40min-point, but note that it's steep and can be slippery underfoot. Keeping to the longer track, ignore another track heading left uphill on a hairpin bend (**2h 30min**) and continue downhill on the main track, to a T-junction with an asphalt road. Turn right here, keeping a long wooden fence on your left as you walk past an enormous pink villa. At **2h40min** you pass a rough track to the right — the end of the short-cut route.

You now pass fruit groves and a large patch of prickly pears, then reach a T-junction (**2h48min**). Turn right and continue to descend towards the dam. There are a few houses by the side of this road, each with superb views — when there is water in the dam. As you round a left hand bend, with a dirt road joining from the right, notice a NATURE TRAIL CAR PARK opposite (**3h**, Picnic 25a). This is the starting point for the Short walk.

Continue left around the bend. After a U-bend, let yourself be tempted by a sign inviting you to head up left to the café in **Phinikaria** (**3h15min**) — where the beer and the views are thoroughly recommended (unfortunately it's closed on Mondays). Afterwards, catch a Line 13 bus at the stop opposite for your return to Limassol.

Of course it's possible to walk on to Germasogia: continue down this road, *watching out for local traffic*. You would cross the dam wall after about an hour. Some 350m

further on you can turn off left on a gravel track (the old road) beside the river. It eventually becomes asphalted; 600m further on, take a road up to the right, to the main road. Turn left to the main square, where buses leave from opposite the café (about 5h).

View down over Germasogia Dam and Phinikaria from the 2h15min-point in the walk. But this may well not be the view that you see! Due to a critical shortage of water, the dam has been bone dry for the past couple of years. Water is being shipped in from mainland Greece, channelled in pipes alongside the dry bed of the Germasogia River, then fed to the dam.

Walk 26: MOUNT MAKHERAS

Distance: 5km/3mi; 1h30min

Grade: moderate, with an ascent/descent of under 200m/650ft overall

Equipment: stout shoes, sunhat, water, picnic

How to get there and return: 🚌 to the Kionia picnic site (from Lemesos via Kellaki and Agii Vavatsinias; from Larnaka via Kalokhorio, Sha, Mathiati and Kataliondas; from Lefkosia via Analiondas).

Tip: The **Kionia nature trail** to Profitis Ilias Monastery is signposted on the other side of the road. The 7km-long trail runs mostly downhill to the monastery (shown on the touring map), with a climb of some 350m/1150ft on the return (14km/87mi return; 5h). The first kilometre of the path is shown on the map and highlighted in yellow.

This journey to the Makheras Forest in the centre of Cyprus affords a stunning view in all directions after a short uphill walk and an energetic scramble along an easy ridge. As one approaches Mount Makheras, from whatever direction, one becomes increasingly aware of the radar weather station on its summit, perched like a huge golf ball on a giant tee.

Below the peak, which is a few kilometres south of Makheras Monastery, we **begin the walk** at the **Kionia** PICNIC SITE, with tables, benches, and barbecue facilities. From the site take steps and then a track up to the main road to the summit and follow it uphill. There is no reason why you should not go all the way to the top for the magnificent panorama seen from just outside the gates to the radar station.

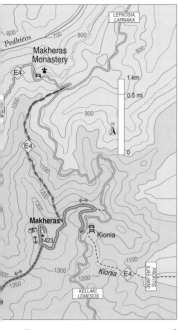

But the main walk continues from a point on the left of the road, less than 200m/yds below the gates (near a gnarled tree), where you climb over the roadside barrier and scramble briefly down the bank, to head for the obvious ridge. Seen from the tree, the scramble looks easier than it is, but it is not difficult for fit walkers.

After some **30min** come to a first CAIRN and, 500m/yds beyond that, another CAIRN (**45min**) — a beautiful high place where one feels as if all Cyprus is spread below you.

Retrace your steps to the **Kionia** PICNIC SITE (**1h30min**), and perhaps call at Makheras Monastery, where there is a seasonal café.

Makheras Monastery, second in importance only to Kykko, was founded in 1148, but burned down in 1530 and again in 1892. Most of what the visitor sees today dates from 1900, but the monastery is a very peaceful and beautiful retreat, especially when the almond trees blossom in February. Views from its terraces are quite impressive. In the 1950s, the EOKA organisation had a hide-out in a nearby cave, where second-in-command Gregoris Afxentiou died after a skirmish with British troops. The monastery, like Kykko, has a wealth of icons — including the one said to have inspired its founding.

Walk 27: STAVROVOUNI MONASTERY

Distance: 4km/2.5mi; 2h

Grade: moderate but steep ascent/descent of 300m/1000ft on a sometimes-overgrown path; avoid in wet weather. *No shade*

Equipment: stout shoes, sunhat, water, picnic, long trousers; optional trekking pole(s)

How to get there and return: 🚗 car or taxi to Stavrovouni (a reasonable taxi journey from Larnaka if sharing). Park/alight at the 'Spithoudia' signpost (see below, paragraph 3). Or Lemesos–Lefkosia 🚌 (Timetable A5) to/from the Stavrovouni turn-off (add 5km/3mi overall).

Special note: Men must wear long trousers to enter Stavrovouni or Agia Varvara, and women are not allowed inside either monastery, nor is photography permitted, but the views from the car park are still superb.

For no other reason than to experience the sheer magnificence of the views from the top, the ascent to Stavrovouni, whether on foot or the easy way, is a must for anyone visiting Cyprus. A grand sweep of the eyes round all points of the compass takes in distant mountains, a whole spectrum of landscape colours and dozens of villages and vineyards.

On three sides, Stavrovouni ('Mountain of the Holy Cross') is almost sheer, but the fourth side is negotiable by the sturdy of foot. Approach is via the old Lefkosia–Lemesos road, or a turn-off from the A1 motorway. The last few miles are hardly a delight, distinguished by a stone-crushing plant and the high-profile presence of an army camp. 'No photography' signs abound. But once this is all behind you, the magic begins.

By vehicle or on foot, head first for the smaller monastery of **Agia Varvara** (bee-keeping and icon-painting) and a point 150m/yds beyond, where the E4 leaves the road to the left. Either follow this or go on for another 150m to where a sign indicates 'SPITHOUDIA' to the right

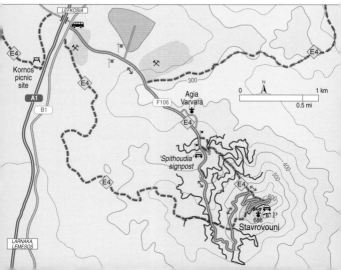

Stavrovouni Monastery: entrance and icons

and there is good parking. Then **start the walk** on the track opposite: follow it for 150m/yds, to pass a small PUMPING STATION on your left. Go right at the Y-fork just beyond it and, 35m/yds further on, take the narrow path rising sharply to the right, joining the E4.

All you have to do now is climb steadily to heaven! The way is steep and rough and not always distinct, but a useful guide is to keep a NARROW PIPE which runs to the top in view. Progress is helped by an occasional levelling-off of the path. When the path touches on hairpin bends in the motor road, look for the contination off to the left. Depending on your scrambling ability, you should reach the summit (688m/2250ft) and **Stavrovouni Monastery** in about **45min**.

Your reward, at the top, is the finest panorama on Cyprus (Picnic 27). The monastery itself is worth looking at, but it should be noted that women visitors are not allowed inside. Stavrovouni is regarded as the oldest monastery on Cyprus, founded by St Helena circa 330, and among its artefacts is a piece of 'the true cross', now encased in silver. The monks are not unwelcoming to (male) visitors, but they are a strict, ascetic group, more interested in devotions than in running a tourist pavilion. Fruit is sometimes available from a stall near the gate, and there are toilet facilities.

The way back down is a choice of either retracing one's footsteps or walking down the motor road. You should be back at the 'SPITHOUDIA' sign at around **2h**, but more if you linger at the top … and who would not?

Walk 28: AROUND CAPE KITI

Distance: 11km/6.8mi; 3h

Grade: easy, level walking, mostly on lanes and tracks, some stretches along the pebbly beach. *No shade, best done from November to April*

Equipment: stout shoes, sunhat, water, picnic, bathing things

How to get there and return: 🚌 to Kiti (Car tour 6). On entering Kiti from the Larnaka direction do not turn right towards the famous Panagia Angeloktistos church. Instead continue into the village centre and look for the other, tiny, church in the village square. Park in the car park directly opposite. Or 🚐 to/from Kiti (Timetable C8).

Shorter circuit: Lighthouse — Agios Leonidos — Perivolia — Kiti Tower — lighthouse (8km/5mi; 2h15min; easy). Access by 🚌 to Kiti lighthouse ('Faros'). Follow the main walk from the 1h26min-point to the 2h28min-point. Go straight on (right), eventually heading south towards the lighthouse. After just over 350m/yds turn left on a road signposted to Larnaka; you'll see the watchtower ahead. The road passes between fields. Join the main walk at the 35min-point, as it comes in from the left, and follow it back to the lighthouse (2h15min). There is also a 🚐 to Perivolia (Timetable C9).

Panagia Angeloktistos ('built by angels') is a must for visitors to the Larnaka area. So before setting off, be sure to admire the beautiful mosaic of the Virgin Mary in the apse. This walk is for those who enjoy taking in the ambience of Cyprus through a gentle stroll. In truth it is a long stroll, but is basically flat. Features are a Venetian watchtower, a lighthouse and a charismatic church with an interesting cemetery. In addition you will see many tourists, expatriates and Cypriots, at leisure, and you may surprise some of them on the beach in less than formal attire!

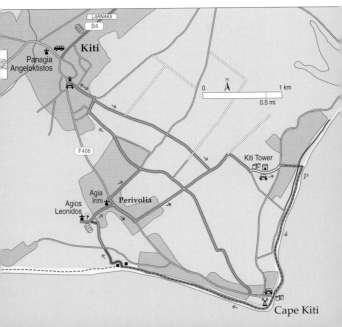

Right: the beautifully-kept church and cemetery of Agios Leonidos outside Perivolia. Below: Kiti Tower, dating from the 15th century, is fenced off — making photography difficult.

Start the walk in **Kiti**, at the tiny CHURCH in the market square. Ignore the F406 road signed to the lighthouse and Perivolia, instead walk out of town down SYNERGASIAS STREET (from the southeast corner of the square), passing the KITI TOWN CLINIC on your right. After 450m/yds turn right towards 'PERIVOLIA'; then, after just 40m/yds, take the first left onto a country road. The watchtower, which is your first objective, is visible directly ahead above the trees. With cultivated fields all around, cross another road, heading slightly to the left (**25min**). After crossing a track, you reach a T-junction (**35min**). *(The Short walk comes in from the right here.)* Turn left and follow the road round a bend to the right. Take the second track off left, 350m/yds past the bend, to rise up to **Kiti Tower** (**48min**), a Venetian watchtower.

Admire the tower and the views towards Larnaka Bay, and then continue on the motorable track to an asphalt road. Cross this and enter a large holiday complex. Go between the rows of villas directly ahead on a pedestrian walkway, to get to the BEACH (**56min**). Turn right and either walk on the beach itself or the 'promenade' (just an unmade road), with fields on the right. On approaching another resort you will have to use the beach, now sandy but compact, until you reach the LIGHTHOUSE (**1h26min**).

Continue round the headland on the pebbly beach. (Or, if the sea is high, take one of the uphill paths cutting across the headland by walking a short distance past the lighthouse and a taverna; then, when you reach a white statue at the entrance to a municipal park, turn left past the swings and follow the path back to the beach to continue.) Some of the new seafront developments here have gardens which reach almost to the sea, so you may have to dodge the waves from time to time!

As the seaside villas start to thin out, look for two villas, each with SMALL JETTIES (**2h**). Turn inland between these villas and walk a few metres across open ground, then turn left on SPATHARIKOU STREET. After a few metres, turn right on PAVLOU KOUNDOURGIOTI. Follow this road past some houses and open fields to a crossroads (**2h13min**). You have been able to see a church for some time, and you are now heading straight for it — perhaps guided by bee-eaters and a red kite. Cross this road and take another road towards the church, eventually turning left on a track. Beautifully maintained **Agios Leonidos** (**2h19min**) is a tranquil resting place.

When you have wandered around and enjoyed this setting, continue on the road past the CEMETERY, signed to LARNAKA. Keep straight on and, just past **Agia Irini** on the left, turn left on 'taverna street' (the F406) in **Perivolia** (**2h28min**). *(The Short walk ignores the delights of the tavernas and continues ahead here.)* At the end of the 100m-long pedestrianised zone devoted to the pleasures of the table, turn right and continue straight on for just under 600m/yds, to a crossroads (**2h38min**). Turn left on ANISTAFIOS AVENUE and follow this suburban street through houses and into open fields. After another 600m turn left on CHRISTOFOROUS PAPANIKOLOU; then, 500m further on, right on ELLADUS STREET. Pass the road you took to Kiti Tower on your right and, at the T-junction 40m ahead, turn left, retracing your steps to the tiny CHURCH in **Kiti** (**3h**).

Panagia Angeloktistos

Walk 29: AGIA NAPA • CAPE GRECO • PROTARAS

Distance: 14km/8.7mi; 4h

Grade: quite easy, but with tricky stretches over razor-sharp rocks

Equipment: boots (ankle protection is *essential* in the latter part of the walk), sunhat, water, picnic, swimming things

How to get there: 🚌 to Agia Napa (Timetables A7, C7). Local buses also serve the Agia Napa/Protaras/Paralimni area (Timetables D3, D4; re-check times at a tourist office)

To return: 🚌 local Agia Napa/Protaras/Paralimni (Timetables D3, D4)

Short walk: This walk can be shortened at almost any point by reaching the coast road and flagging down a bus, or calling for a taxi from any of the hotels. Stout shoes will suffice as far as Kermia Beach.

The far reaches of any island always hold fascination for the traveller, and this southeastern corner of Cyprus is no exception. It is easily accessible too — Agia Napa is one of the island's most popular tourist centres. This walk takes in sandy beaches, quiet coves, a radar-topped headland and an attractively-sited church.

Begin the walk on LEOFOROS KRYOU NEROU in **Agia Napa**, just north of the GRECIAN SANDS HOTEL. Joining the E4, take the track that leads seawards, offering a pleasing view over Agia Napa beach within two minutes. Then simply keep close to the sea and head eastwards (Picnic 29), experiencing a palm-planted 'promenade', little sandy beaches, rocky inlets and, at about **40min**, **Kermia Beach** and its apartments.

A few minutes beyond here, the promenade ends and the going gets tricky if you want to keep to the coast, rather than follow the inland path. It is not difficult to pick a way through the sharp-edged rocks underfoot, but great care should be taken to avoid ankle injury. Progress here will be slower, but you will have a fine view of inlets where waves crash into sea caves (see page 118).

At around **1h15min**, perhaps sooner, you will approach the dominant HEADLAND which has been in view throughout the walk (but it's not Cape Greco!). Better here to move away from the sea, and join the track ahead to the left. A worthwhile detour at this point is to enjoy one of the Forestry Department nature trails on this headland, now incorporated into the E4 (highlighted on our map with dashed green lines); you'll have splendid views over Cape Greco and along to Agia Napa. From the top of this flat headland (93m) one can even pick out Stavrovouni (Walk 27) in the west and — on very clear days — see the mountains on the far side of the Med. It's just 1km by track from the top to the main road, where you could catch a bus and end the walk.

If you are pressing on to Cape Greco, keep to (or rejoin) the route at the base of the headland, round it, then catch a first glimpse of the cape with its lighthouse and the relay masts of Radio Monte Carlo. A little further on, look to a military radar installation high on the left. Following the E4, keep to the right of a cultivated area, climb a low hill, then take a track down to the **Cape Greco** road. You'll have a closer view to the radio masts here, but a locked gate prevents access to the cape itself.

Cross the road and make for the eastern side of the

cape, where you'll find the picturesque little church of **Agii Anargyri** (**2h**). You could end the walk here, by heading up the road and catching a bus back to Agia Napa on the E307. Otherwise, follow the E4 path off to the right, along the edge of a not-very-high cliff, to sandy **Konnos Bay** (visible from Agii Anargyri).

At about **2h15min** come to a road zigzagging down to the bay, but don't follow it down to the beach; cross a BRIDGE on the left and follow a track overlooking the beach (there may be a sign for 'CYCLOP'S CAVE here).

Looking back to Agia Napa from the sea caves east of Kermia Beach

Beyond another, more rocky bay down to the right, bear left for a moment to observe **Cyclop's Cave** in the hillside (**2h45min**), but return to follow the edge of the cliff. Vertigo is a small risk, but easily avoided. Some miles off the cape there is believed to lie the wreck of a 15th-century Genoese ship, as yet undiscovered.

Beyond the boulders and undergrowth of an old quarry, you come to a broad track heading left past an improvised parking area, but keep seawards for a minute or two, then head left to walk parallel with the shore, about 100m/yds inland. To the left are a few houses, ahead is a WINDMILL, and away to the right a jagged, rocky area leading to the sea. Explore it if you wish, but watch your ankles!

From here, progress is over a completely flat coastal strip. Beyond the windmill, you could head up to the junction of the E306/E307 for a bus, if you're flagging. Otherwise, make your way past ever-diminishing patches of farmland interspersed with new resorts, over rocks, and round sandy inlets, until you reach **Protaras** after about **4h**.

Walk 30: AGIA NAPA TO PROFITIS ILIAS

See map pages 116-117; see also photographs on pages 40, 116, 117

Distance: 8km/5mi; 2h

Grade: quite easy; little climbing

Equipment: walking boots or stout shoes, sunhat, water, picnic

How to get there: 🚌 to Agia Napa (Timetables A7, C7). Local buses also serve the Agia Napa/Protaras/Paralimni area (Timetables D3,D4; re-check times at a tourist office)

To return: 🚌 local Agia Napa/Protaras/Paralimni (Timetables D3, D4)

Short walk: Agii Saranta (2km/1.2mi; 45min return). 🚗 drive the first part of the walk, along the rough road, and park short of the transmitter tower. Then use the notes below from the 35min- to the 50min-point and return the same way.

Tip: There is a signposted CTO trail running *inland* between Konnos Bay and Profitis Ilias via Agios Ioannis and Agii Saranta (see yellow highlighting on our map). We pick up this trail just southwest of Agii Saranta and follow it to Profitis Ilias. The E4 uses part of this route.

This walk explores the gentle agricultural hills behind Agia Napa and Protaras. Prise yourself away from the golden beaches and you'll find that some modest exertion reveals a different world... of wind-powered wells, rich red soil producing a harvest of vegetables, quaint little churches, and a few stony tracks waiting to be explored.

The walk can be done in either direction, but it is easier to locate the **start at Agia Napa**. From the centre, walk north on the PARALIMNI ROAD, and turn right (with the E4) just past the POLICE STATION on a road that leads in **10min** or less to the community STADIUM. Turn left soon after passing this, and continue round the edge of PLAYING FIELDS. Ignore the motor track past the playing fields; take

Cyprus is surrounded by water but, surprisingly, fish are not plentiful. Fishing boats do operate — here's one at Cape Greco — and specialities you can expect to find in restaurants include swordfish, red mullet, octopus, and the ubiquitous squid or 'kalamares'.

the *next* track to the right, heading towards a radio transmitter mast in the middle distance. A short way from the mast, at about **35min**, the motor track makes a definite left turn. At this point, you should turn off right on a path through an area of low trees and come to an open area from where there are views to Cape Greco.

The path joins the CTO/E4 trail, a motor track which you follow left, to **Agii Saranta** (**50min**; Picnic 30). This most unusual, tiny church is set in a cave, and its only light comes from the dome on the hillside above it. Inside you will find evidence of a latter-day icon painter at work, and the familar candles.

Continue on the CTO trail beyond Agii Saranta for about 10 minutes, to a fork where 'Panagia' is signposted to the right; keep straight ahead for 'PROFITIS ILIAS', with the transmitter mast away to the left. At **1h05min** or less you should be getting views off to the right — to the imposing church of Profitis Ilias on its rocky perch, with Protaras behind it. Keep to the track, with the transmitter mast away to the left, and come to an ELECTRICITY WORKS. Turn sharp right off the main track here, and follow a faint track towards and then past a cylindrical WATER TANK. When asphalt comes underfoot at a villa development, keep downhill, then climb the steps to **Profitis Ilias** (**2h**). Views from the church and its pedestal are pleasing; the church is modern but very attractive inside and out. From Profitis Ilias descend steps to the main coast road and pick up a bus or taxi.

120

SERVICE TAXI AND BUS TIMETABLES

Below are relevant destinations served by public transport. The number after the place name is the **timetable number**. Timetables follow on the next 12 pages, but *do* download the latest timetables for any service you may use just before you travel. You can usually get all the relevant information you need (with interactive maps) at **www.cyprusbybus.com**. But for rural and suburban services, if cyprusbybus.com does not have the timetable, you will have to log on to the individual operators' websites shown for the various areas. Departure points for buses and service taxis are shown on the town plans (see pages 8-13) and the walking maps.

Agia Napa
— Larnaka C7, D1, D3
— Lefkosia A7, D2
— Paralimni D1-D4
Agios Georgios — Pafos E6
Agios Neophytos — Pafos E9
Agros — Lemesos B8
Arkhimandrita — Pafos E10
Baths of Aphrodite — Polis F1
Coral Bay — Pafos E8
Germasogia — Lemesos B10
Governor's Beach — Lemesos B12
Kakopetria — Lefkosia A8
Kellaki — Lemesos B11
Kissonerga — Pafos E7
Kiti — Larnaka C8
Lakki — Polis F1
Larnaka (Larnaca)
all destinations C1-C10
— Agia Napa C7
— Kiti C8
— Lefkosia A1, A4, C1, C4
— Lemesos B2, B6, C2, C5
— Pafos C3, E3
— Paralimni C7
— Perivolia C9
— Protaras C7
— tourist beach C10
Lefkosia (Nicosia)
all destinations A1-A10
— Agia Napa D2
— Kakopetria A8
— Larnaka A1, A4, C1, C4
— Lemesos A2, A5, A12, B1, B4
— Pafos A3, A6, E2
— Paralimni A7, D2
— Platres A8
— Protaras A7, D2
— Troodos A10
Lemesos (Limassol)
all destinations B1-B12
— Agros B8
— Germasogia B10
— Governor's Beach B12
— Kellaki B11

— Larnaka B2, B6, C2, C5
— Lefkosia A2, A5, B1, B4
— Pafos B3, B5, E1, E4
— Phinikaria B11
— Platres and Troodos B7
— Prodhromos B7
Pafos (Paphos)
all destinations E1-E9
— Agios Georgios E6
— Agios Neophytos E9
— Arkhimandrita E10
— Coral Bay E8
— Kissonerga E7
— Larnaka C3, E3
— Lefkosia A3, A6, E2
— Lemesos B3, B5, E1, E4
— Polis E5
— Tala E9
Paralimni
— Agia Napa D1-D4
— Larnaka C7, D1, D3
— Lefkosia A7
— Protaras D1-D4
Petra tou Romiou
— Lemesos B5
— Pafos E4
Phinikaria — Lemesos B11
Pissouri
— Lemesos B5
— Pafos E4
Platres
— Lefkosia A8
— Lemesos B7
Polis
— Baths of Aphrodite F1
— Lakki F1
— Pafos E5
Prodhromos
— Lefkosia A8
— Lemesos B7
Protaras
— Agia Napa D1-D4
— Larnaka C7
— Lefkosia A7
— Paralimni D1-D4
Troodos — Lefkosia A10

121

No	Itinerary	Company	Address or Location

Services from LEFKOSIA (Nicosia)

SERVICE TAXIS (all are operated by 'Travel & Expre

No	Itinerary	Company	Address or Location
A1	Lefkosia to LARNAKA	Intercity Service Taxi	Municipal Parking — Place Kolokasi (Podokatoro)
A2	Lefkosia to LEMESOS	*as A1 above*	*As A1 above*
A3	Lefkosia to PAFOS	*as A1 above*	*As A1 above*

BUS SERVICES — INTERCITY (all are operated by

No	Itinerary	Company	Address or Location
A4	Lefkosia to LARNAKA	Intercity Buses	Solomos Square
A5	Lefkosia to LEMESOS	Intercity Buses	Solomos Square
A6	Lefkosia to PAFOS	Intercity Buses	Solomos Square
A7	Lefkosia to AGIA NAPA and PARALIMNI	Intercity Buses	Solomos Square

BUS SERVICES — RURAL AND SUBURBAN (all

No	Itinerary	Company	Address or Location
A8	Lefkosia to PLATRES (Route: Platres—Prodhromos—Pedhoulas)	OSEL	Solomos Square
	PLATRES to Lefkosia (Route: Pedhoulas—Prodhromos—Platres)	OSEL	for departure point enquire at tourist office
A9	Lefkosia to KAKOPETRIA	OSEL	Solomos Square
	KAKOPETRIA to Lefkosia	OSEL	Kakopetria village
A10	Lefkosia to TROODOS	OSEL	Solomos Square
	TROODOS to Lefkosia	OSEL	Troodos main street

Telephone No	Winter Timetable (Summer services may be more frequent)

— www.travelexpress.com.cy)

7777 7474 or 22-730888	*Daily*, every half hour from 06.00 to 18.00 (17.00 Sat/Sun)
As A1 above	*As A1 above*
As A1 above	*As A1 above*

Intercity — www.intercity-buses.com)

8000 7789 or 24-643493	*Mon-Fri*: 06.00, 07.30, 08.45, 09.30, 10.30, 13.00, 14.00, 14.30, 16.00, 17.30, 18.30, 20.00 *Sat/Sun*: 08.00, 09.30-11.30 (every hour), 13.00, 16.30, 18.00, 19.30
8000 7789 or 24-643493	*Mon-Fri*: 06.00, 07.00, 08.30-14.30 (hourly), 16.30, 18.30, 20.30 *Sat/Sun*: 07.00, 08.45, 10.30, 13.00-21.00 (every two hours)
8000 7789 or 24-643493	*Mon-Fri*: 05.00, 08.30, 11.00, 14.30, 18.00; *Sat/Sun*: 08.00, 12.00, 15.00, 18.00
7777 7755 or 22-468088	*Mon-Fri*: 08.15, 11.30, 15.00, 17.00 *Sat/Sun*: 09.00, 10.00, 18.30

operated by OSEL (www.osel.com.cy)

7777 7755 or 22-468088	*Mon-Sat only*: 12.15
7777 7755 or 22-468088	*Mon-Sat only*: 06.00 (does not call at Platres on Saturdays unless reserved in advance)
7777 7755 or 22-468088	*Mon-Fri*: 06.00, 10.20, 11.30, 13.00, 14.00, 14.30, 15.30, 16.20, 16.45, 17.30, 18.00 *Sat*: 11.30, 13.00, 14.00, 17.30 *Sun*: 08.00, 17.00 *(18.00 in July and August)*
	Mon-Fri: 05.00, 05.45, 06.10, 06.30, 06.45, 08.00, 13.30, 14.30 *Sat*: 06.00, 06.45, 08.00, 14.30 *Sun*: 06.00, 16.30 *(July and August)*
7777 7755 or 22-468088	*Mon-Fri*: 10.20; *Sat*: 11.30 *From Troodos to Platres:* 15.15 *Mon-Sat*: 06.30 *(also 17.00 in July and August)*

No	Itinerary	Company	Address or Location

Services from LEMESOS (Limassol)

SERVICE TAXIS (all are operated by 'Travel &

B1	Lemesos to LEFKOSIA	Intercity Service Taxi	Vasileos Pavlou
B2	Lemesos to LARNAKA	*as B1 above*	*as B1 above*
B3	Lemesos to PAFOS	*as B1 above*	*as B1 above*

BUS SERVICES — INTERCITY (all are operated by

B4	Lemesos to LEFKOSIA	Intercity Buses	new port, Debenhams and St Raphael
B5	Lemesos to PAFOS	Intercity Buses	new port, old port, St George Havousas
B6	Lemesos to LARNAKA	Intercity Buses	new port, Debenhams St Raphael

BUS SERVICES — RURAL AND SUBURBAN

B7	Lemesos to PLATRES and TROODOS *TROODOS/PLATRES to Lemesos*	EMEL Bus 64 EMEL Bus 64	EMEL central station, 194 Leontiou Troodos square/ Platres centre
B8	Lemesos to AGROS *AGROS to Lemesos*	EMEL Buses 66, 50 EMEL	EMEL central station, 194 Leontiou Agros village centre
B9	Lemesos to AMATHUS (hotel area) *AMATHUS (hotel area) to Lemesos*	EMEL Buses 30, 31 EMEL Buses 30, 31	New port and all stops along the coastal road Hotel Meridien
B10	Lemesos to PHINIKARIA and GERMASOGIA *GERMASOGIA to Lemesos*	EMEL Bus 13 EMEL Bus 13	EMEL station, Lambrou Porfira main square in Germasogia
B11	Lemesos to KELLAKI *KELLAKI to Lemesos*	Bus 80 Bus 80	EMEL, 194 Leontiou Kellaki square
B12	Lemesos to GOVERNOR *BEACH to Lemesos*	Bus 95A Bus 95A	EMEL, Old Port Governor's Beach

Telephone No	Winter Timetable (Summer services may be more frequent)

Express' — www.travelexpress.com.cy)

7777 7474 or 25-877666	*Daily,* every half hour from 06.00 to 18.00 (17.00 Sat/Sun)
as B1 above	*as B1 above*
as B1 above	*as B1 above*

Intercity — www.intercity-buses.com)

8000 7789 or 24-643493	*Mon-Fri:* 05.30, 06.00, 07.30, 09.00, 10.30-14.30 (every hour), 16.30-20.30 (every two hours) *Sat/Sun:* 07.00, 08.45, 10.30, 13.00-21.00 (every hour), 21.00
8000 7789 or 24-643493	*Mon-Fri:* 06.15, 07.30, 09.30, 11.30, 13.00, 15.00, 16.00, 17.30, 19.30, 21.00 *Sat/Sun:* 06.00, 07.45, 11.00, 14.30, 17.30, 21.00
8000 7789 or 24-643493	*Mon-Fri:* 06.00, 08.00, 09.00, 10.30, 11.30, 13.30, 14.30, 16.00, 18.00, 19.30 *Sat/Sun:* 08.30, 10.30, 11.30, 14.00, 16.00, 18.00

(operated by EMEL — www.limassolbuses.com)

7777 8121	*Daily:* 09.30
	From Troodos: 08.45 (Mon-Fri only), 15.30 *From Platres:* 07.20, 09.00 (not Sun), 15.45
7777 8121	*Mon-Sat:* 07.30, 12.00, 13.30, 16.15, 18.15 *Sun:* 11.00, 17.00 *Mon-Sat:* 06.00, 07.00, 09.00; *Sun:* 09.40, 16.10
7777 8121	Service operates year round along the coast road approximately every 15 minutes
	Service operates year round along the coast road approximately every 15 minutes
7777 8121	*Mon-Fri:* 08.00and approx. hourly until 19.05; *Sat:* 08.00, 09.00, 10.00, 11.00; *Sun:* 09.15, 10.15
	Mon-Fri: 08.00and approx. hourly until 16.30; *Sat:* 14.05, 15.25, 16.45; *Sun:* 15.00, 16.00, 17.00
7777 8121	*Mon-Fri:* 11.50, 13.30; *Sat:* 11.50; *Sun:* 10.10
	Mon-Fri: 15.20; *Sat:* 06.15; *Sun:* 15.20
7777 8121	*Daily:* 10.00
	Daily: 16.00

No	Itinerary	Company	Address or Location

Services from LARNAKA

SERVICE TAXIS (all are operated by 'Travel &

No	Itinerary	Company	Address or Location
C1	Larnaka to LEFKOSIA	Inercity Service Taxi	Corner of Kilkis and Kitiou streets
C2	Larnaka to LEMESOS	*as C1 above*	*As C1 above*
C3	Larnaka to PAFOS	*as C1 above*	*As C1 above*

BUS SERVICES — INTERCITY (all are operated by

No	Itinerary	Company	Address or Location
C4	Larnaka to LEFKOSIA	Intercity Buses	Phinikoudes Avenue (near the Kimon statu
C5	Larnaka to LEMESOS	Intercity Buses	Phinikoudes Avenue (near the Kimon statu
	Larnaka to PAFOS — *Service via Lemesos; see Timetables C5 and B.*		
C6	**Larnaka to AGIA NAPA/ PROTARAS/ PARALIMNI**	Intercity Buses	Phinikoudes Avenue (near the Kimon statu

BUS SERVICES — RURAL AND SUBURBAN

No	Itinerary	Company	Address or Location
C7	**Larnaka to AGIA NAPA/ PROTARAS/ PARALIMNI**	Osea Bus 711	bus stop opposite the police station, Leofore Archbishop Makariou
	PARALIMNI/PROTARAS/AGIA NAPA to Larnaka: see Timetab		
C8	**Larnaka to KITI** (Angeloktistos Church)	Zinonas, Bus No 419	Phinikoudes Avenue (near the Kimon statu
	KITI to Larnaka	Bus No 419; *Kiti is also served by Bus 407*	Kiti village (Archbishop Makariou
C9	**Larnaka to PERIVOLIA**	*as Timetable C8*	
	PERIVOLIA to Larnaka	*as Timetable C8*	
C10	**Larnaka to TOURIST BEACH EAST of Larnaka**	Bus 431 Zinonas	Phinikoudes Avenue (near the Kimon statu
	TOURIST BEACH EAST to Larnaka	Bus 431 Zinonas	tourist beach east of Larnaka

Telephone No	Winter Timetable (Summer services may be more frequent)

Express' — www.travelexpress.com.cy)

Telephone No	Winter Timetable
7777 7474 or 24-661010	*Daily,* every half hour from 06.00 to 18.00 (17.00 Saturdays and Sundays) *as above*
As C1 above	*As C1 above*
As C1 above	*As C1 above*

Intercity — www.intercity-buses.com)

Telephone No	Winter Timetable
7000 77 89 or 24-643493	*Mon-Fri:* 06.30, 07.15, 09.30-10.30 (every hour), 11.00, 12.00, 13.00, 14.15, 16.30, 18.30, 19.30 *Sat/Sun:* 06.30, 08.00, 09.00, 10.30, 13.00, 16.00-20.00 (every two hours)
7000 77 89 or 24-643493	*Mon-Fri:* 06.00, 08.00, 09.00, 10.30, 11.30, 13.30, 14.30, 16.00, 18.00, 19.30 *Sat/Sun:* 08.30, 10.30, 11.30, 14.00, 16.00, 18.00
7000 77 89 or 24-643493	*Mon-Fri:* 06.00, 07.45, 09.15, 10.00, 11.00, 13.00, 14.30, 16.00, 18.00, 19.30 *Sat/Sun:* 08.00, 10.00, 11.30, 14.30, 16.00, 17.30

(operated by Zinonas — www.zinonasbuses.com) and Osea — www.osea.com.cy)

Telephone No	Winter Timetable
8000 7744 or 23-819090	*Mon-Fri:* 08.15, 10.30, 11.15, 13.45, 16.30, 18.30 *Sat/Sun:* 10.00, 13.30, 15.30, 18.00
8000 7744 or 24-665531	*Mon-Fri:* 06.20, 07.30, 08.30, 09.15, 10.00, 12.00, 14.00, 15.30, 17.00, 18.30, 20.00 *Sat/Sun:* 11.30, 14.00, 15.30, 17.00, 18.30, 20.00
	Mon-Fri: 05.45, 07.40, 09.15, 10.00, 10.45, 11.15, 12.35, 14.45, 16.15, 17.45, 19.15 *Sat/Sun:* 09.15, 10.45, 12.15, 13.15, 14.45, 16.15
8000 7744 or 24-665531	*Mon-Fri:* 08.30, 10.00, 12.00, 15.00, 16.00, 18.00 *Sat/Sun:* 08.30, 10.00, 12.00, 14.30, 15.30
8000 7744 or 24-665531	*Mon-Fri:* 08.00, 09.30, 11.30, 14.30, 15.30, 17.30 *Sat/Sun:* 08.00, 09.30, 11.30, 14.00, 15.00, 16.00

No	Itinerary	Company	Address or Location

Services from Agia Napa, Paralimni, Protaras

BUS SERVICES — INTERCITY (all are operated b

D1	**Paralimni/Protaras/ Agia Napa to LARNAKA**	Intercity Buses	St George (Paralimni Cape Greco Ave, belo Profitis Ilias (Protara Monastery, Agia Napa
D2	*PARALIMNI and AGIA NAPA to Lefkosia*	Intercity Buses	St George (Paralimni Monastery, Agia Napa

BUS SERVICES — RURAL AND SUBURBAN

D3	**Paralimni/Protaras/ Agia Napa to LARNAKA**	Osea Bus 711	Kappari Avenue (Para Cape Greco Ave, belo Profitis Ilias (Protara Corner Makariou/Eva Floraki (Agia Napa)
	LARNAKA to Agia Napa: see Timetable C7		
D4	**Agia Napa to PARALIMNI (via PROTARAS)**	Osea Bus 101	Corner Makariou/Eva Floraki (Agia Napa) Cape Greco Ave, belo Profitis Ilias (Protara St George (Paralimni Corner of Makariou a
	PARALIMNI to Agia Napa (via PROTARAS)	Osea Bus 102	Ag Georgios Square Cape Greco Ave, belo Profitis Ilias (Protara Corner Makariou/Eva Floraki (Agia Napa)

Telephone No	Winter Timetable (Summer services may be more frequent)

Intercity — www.intercity-buses.com)

7000 77 89 or 24-643493	*Mon-Fri:* 06.00, 07.45, 08.45, 09.30, 10.45, 14.15, 16.00, 17.30, 19.00, 20.30 *Sat/Sun:* 08.00, 10.00, 11.30, 13.00, 14.30, 16.15, 18.30, 20.00
7777 7755 or 22-468088	*Mon-Fri:* 08.00, 10.30, 13.30, 18.30 *Sat/Sun:* 08.00, 10.00, 17.30, 20.30

(operated by Osea — www.osea.com.cy)

8000 7744 or 23-819090	*Mon-Fri:* 08.00, 08.45, 11.00, 14.10, 16.00 *Sat/Sun:* 07.45, 10.30, 13.15, 15.30
8000 7744 or 23-819090	*Mon-Sat:* 09.00, 09.30*, 10.00, 10.30*, 11.00, 11.30*, 12.00, 13.00, 14.00, 14.45*, 16.00, 16.30*, 17.00, 17.30*, 17.45*, 18.00*, 18.30*, 19.00*, 19.30*, 20.00* *Sun:* 09.00*, 10.00*, 11.00*, 12.00*, 13.00*, 14.00*, 16.00*, 17.00* *these buses run May to October only
8000 7744 or 23-819090	*Daily, May-Oct:* 09.00, 09.30*, 10.00, 10.30*, 11.00, 11.30*, 12.00, 13.00, 14.00, 15.00*, 16.00, 16.30*, 17.00, 18.00, 19.00, 20.00* *not on Sundays *Nov-Apr, Mon-Sat only:* 09.00, 10.00, 11.00, 12.00, 13.00, 14.00, 16.00, 17.00

No	Itinerary	Company	Address or Location

Services from PAFOS

SERVICE TAXIS (all are operated by 'Travel &

E1	Pafos to LEMESOS	Intercity Service Taxi	34 Kiniras
E2	Pafos to LEFKOSIA — *as Timetable E1*		
E3	Pafos to LARNAKA — *as Timetable E1*		

BUS SERVICES — INTERCITY (all are operated by

E4	Pafos to LEMESOS	Intercity Buses	Karavella bus station
	Pafos to LEFKOSIA — *Service via Lemesos; see Timetables E4 and*		
	Pafos to LARNAKA — *Service via Lemesos; see Timetable E4 and*		

BUS SERVICES — RURAL AND SUBURBAN

E5	Pafos to POLIS	OSYPA Bus 645	Karavella bus station
	POLIS to Pafos	OSYPA Bus 645	Polis centre
E6	Pafos to AGIOS GEORGIOS	OSYPA Bus 615/6	Kato Pafos harbour bus station (Bus 615 Coral Bay, then chang
	AGIOS GEORGIOS to Pafos	OSYPA Bus 616A or *Bus 616B*	Agios Georgios churc (Bus 616 A or B to Coral Bay, then chang
E7	Pafos to KISSONERGA	OSYPA Bus 607	Karavella station
	KISSONERGA to Pafos	OSYPA Bus 607	Kissonerga church
E8	Pafos to CORAL BAY	OSYPA Bus 615	Kato Pafos harbour bus station
	CORAL BAY to Pafos	OSYPA Bus 615	Coral Bay

Telephone No	Winter Timetable (Summer services may be more frequent)

Express' — www.travelexpress.com.cy)

7777 7474 or 26-923800	*Daily*, every half hour from 06.00 to 18.00 (17.00 Saturdays and Sundays)

Intercity — www.intercity-buses.com)

8000 7789 or 24-643493 or 26-220887	*Mon-Fri:* 06.00, 07.30, 09.00, 10.00, 11.00, 14.30, 15.00, 16.30, 18.00, 19.30 *Sat/Sun:* 07.30, 09.30, 13.00, 16.30, 19.30

(OSYPA; www.PafosBuses.com)

8000 5588 or 26-934252	*Mon-Fri:* 06.20, 08.00, 09.00, 10.00, 11.00, 12.00, 14.00, 15.00, 16.00, 17.00, 18.00 *Sat:* 08.00, 09.00, 10.00, 11.00, 13.00, 15.00, 16.00, 18.00; *Sun:* 10.00, 12.00, 13.00, 14.00, 15.00, 17.00
8000 5588 or 26-934252	*Mon-Fri:* 05.30, 06.30, 08.00, 09.00, 10.00, 11.00, 13.00, 13.45, 15.00, 16.00, 17.00 *Sat:* 08.00, 09.00, 12.00, 14.00, 15.00, 17.00 *Sun:* 09.00, 11.00, 12.00, 13.00, 14.00, 16.00
8000 5588 or 26-934252	*First take Bus 615 to Coral Bay (at least every 15 minutes), then Bus 616A or 616B from Corallia Beach:* 08.30, 09.30, 10.20, 10.30, 11.30, 13.10, 13.30, 14.30, 15.00, 15.30, 16.00, 16.30
as above	every hour from 09.00-12.00 and 14.00-17.00 *daily, from April to November*
8000 5588 or 26-934252	*Mon-Fri:* 06.00, 08.30, 09.50, 11.40, 16.00, 18.00 *Sat:* 07.40, 11.20, 13.40, 16.20 *Mon-Fri:* 10.45, 12.50, 17.00; *Sat:* 14.50, 17.20
8000 5588 or 26-934252	*All year round:* too frequent to list, about every 15 min after 6am until midnight Buses and frequency as above

No	Itinerary	Company	Address or Location
E9	Pafos to AGIOS NEOPHYTOS	OSYPA Bus 604	Karavella station
	AGIOS NEOPHYTOS to Pafos	**OSYPA Bus 604**	the monastery
E10	Pafos to PANO ARKHIMANDRITA	OSYPA Bus 632	Karavella station
	ARKHIMANDRITA to Pafos	OSYPA Bus 632	village centre

Services from POLIS*

BUS SERVICES — RURAL AND SUBURBAN

F1	**Polis to the BATHS OF APHRODITE and LAKKI**	Pafos Transport Bus 622	Kyproleontos Street (opposite the tourist office)
	LAKKI and the BATHS OF APHRODITE to Polis	Pafos Tansport Bus 622	Lakki harbour or restaurant at Baths of Aphrodite

*Note that there are also services from Polis to several of the villages en route in our walks (for instance Kathikas, Akoursos, Theletra, Miliou, Drousseia, the Terras), but at press date timings were inconvenient. All Polis departures are listed on cyprusbybus.com or on PafosBuses.com as well as in the timetables available from the tourist office in Pafos.

NOTES

Telephone No	Winter Timetable (Summer services may be more frequent)
8000 5588 or 26-934252	*Mon-Fri:* 06.30, 09.20, 11.10, 14.20, 16.00, 17.40 *Sat:* 08.10, 10.50, 15.00, 17.40
	Mon-Fri: 07.10, 10.00, 11.50, 15.00, 16.40, 18.20 *Sat:* 08.50, 11.30, 15.40, 18.20
8000 5588 or 26-934252	*Mon-Sat:* 06.15, 10.14.10 (13.30 on Saturdays)
8000 5588 or 26-934252	*Mon-Sat:* 07.40, 10.50, 15.00 (14.20 on Saturdays)

(operated by OSPYA; www.PafosBuses.com)

8000 5588 or 26-934252	*Mon-Fri:* 06.00, then every hour from 08.00-12.00 and from 15.00-18.00 *Sat/Sun:* 06.00, 10.00, 11.00, 12.00, 14.00, 15.00, 18.00
8000 5588 or 26-934252	*Mon-Fri:* 06.30, then every hour from 08.30 to 12.30 and 15.30 to 18.30 *Sat/Sun:* 06.30, 10.30, 11.30, 12.30, 14.30, 15.30, 18.30

NOTES

● Index

Geographical entries only are included in this index. For other entries, ˢ
Contents, page 3. A page number in *italic type* indicates a map reference
page number in **bold type** indicates a photograph or drawing. Both of the
may be in addition to a text reference on the same page. 'TM' refers to t
large-scale walking map on the reverse of the touring map. Transpe
timetables are given on pages 121 to 133.

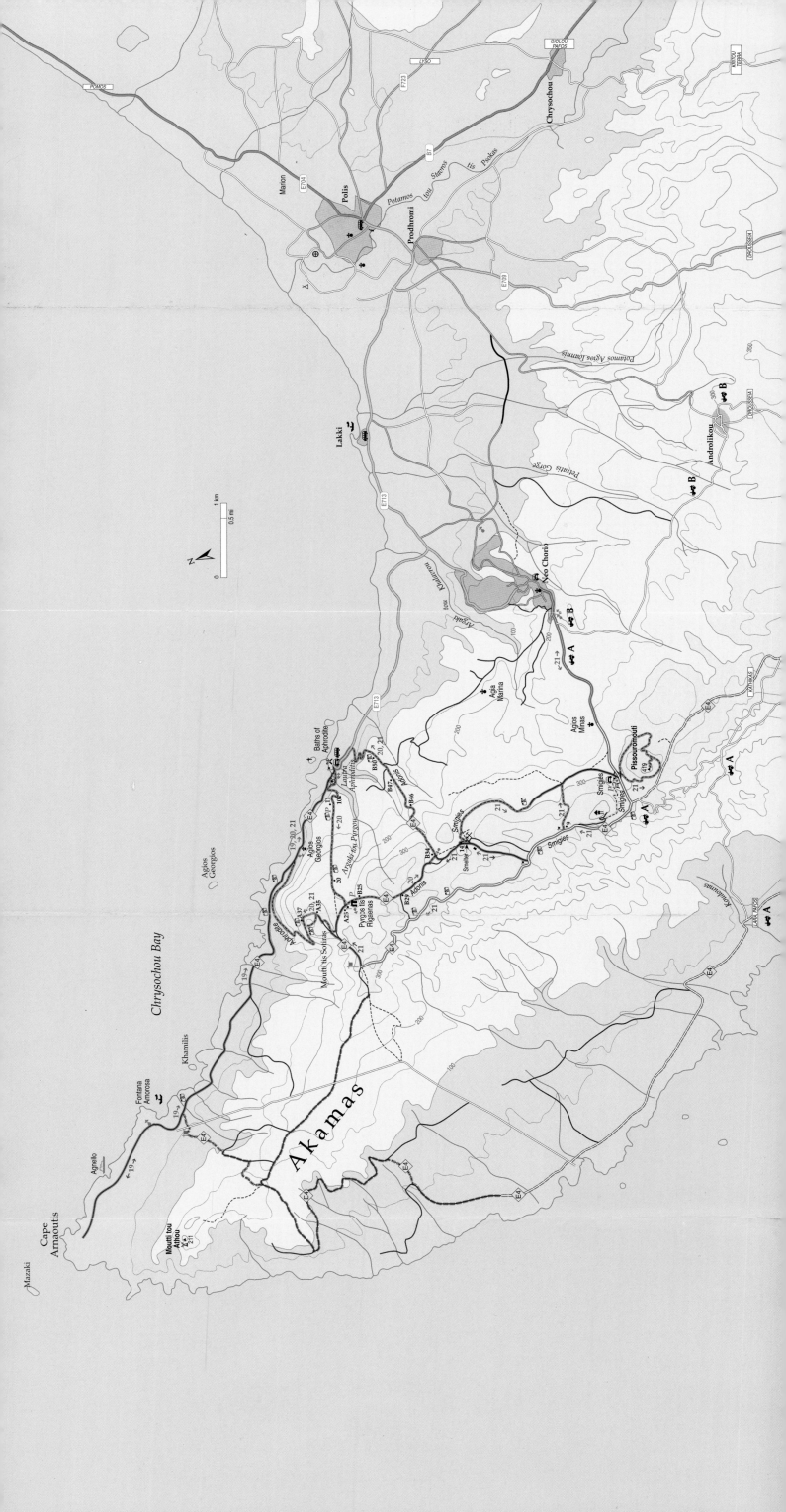

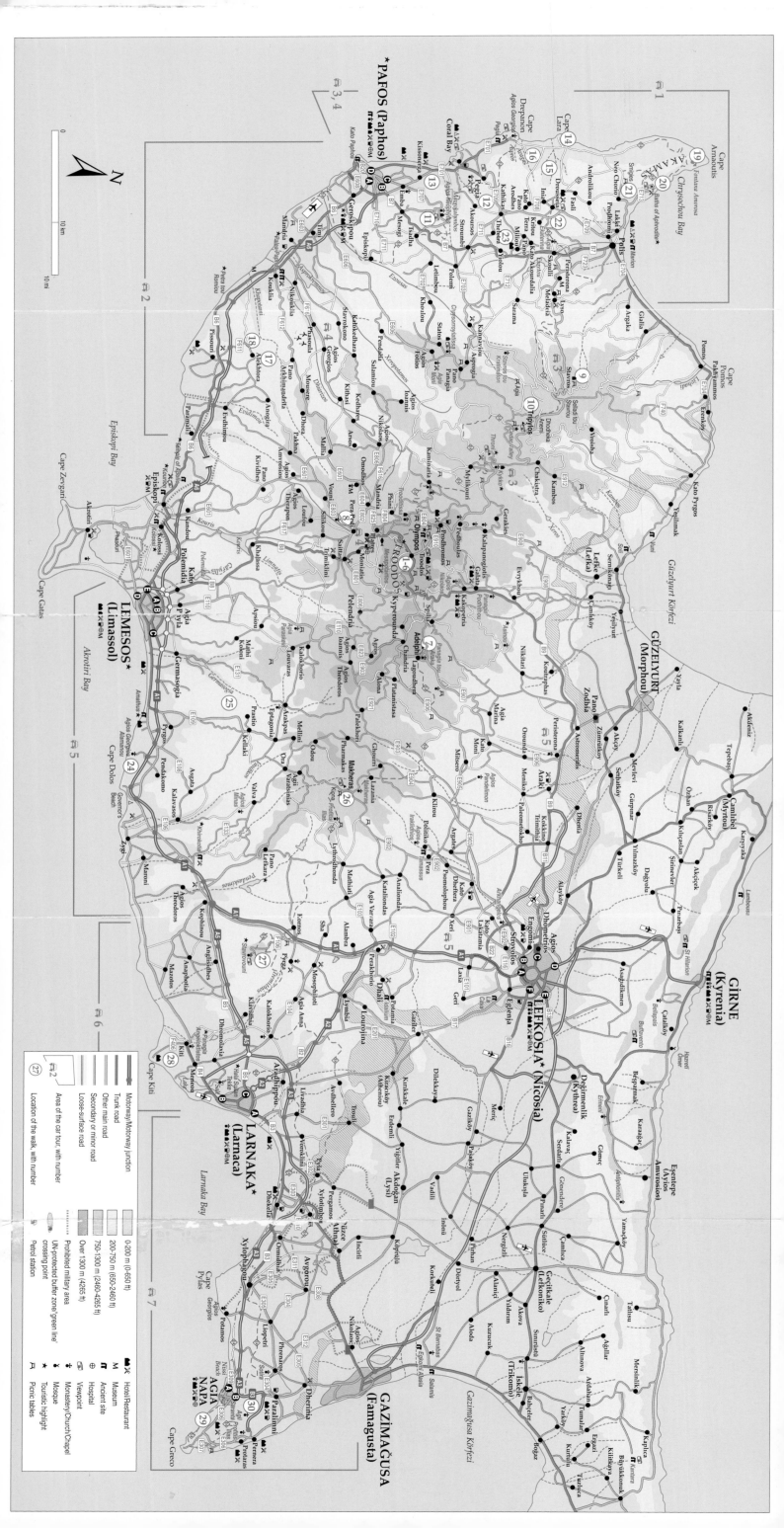